Let's say you're on *Let's Make a Deal!*, when Monty Hall offers you what's behind Door Number One, Door Number Two, or Door Number Three.

Now Monty has promised you that behind one of those doors is the grand prize. Behind the other two doors are lemons.

With great anticipation you pick Door Number Three . . . but instead of opening door Number Three, Monty opens Door Number One to reveal a lemon. Of course, you know what comes next: Monty offers you the choice of sticking with Door Number Three or choosing Door Number Two instead.

What should you do?

You'll find the answer in . . .

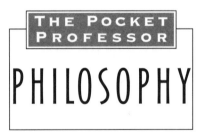

THE POCKET
PROFESSOR

PHILOSOPHY

EVERYTHING YOU NEED TO KNOW ABOUT
PHILOSOPHY

STEVE HERMAN, PH.D.
WITH
GREGG STEBBEN

SERIES EDITOR: DENIS BOYLES

POCKET BOOKS
New York   London   Toronto   Sydney   Tokyo   Singapore

An *Original* Publication of POCKET BOOKS

 POCKET BOOKS, a division of Simon & Schuster Inc.
1230 Avenue of the Americas, New York, NY 10020

Copyright © 1999 by Denis Boyles

Library of Congress Cataloging-in-Publication Data

Herman, Stephen.
　　Everything you want to know about philosophy / Stephen Herman with Gregg Stebben.
　　　　p.　cm.—(The pocket professor)
　　Includes index.
　　ISBN 0-671-53488-2
　　1. Philosophy Introductions.　　I. Stebben, Gregg.　　II. Title.
III. Series.
BD21.H47　1999
100—dc21　　　　　　　　　　　　　　　　　　　　　99-31305
　　　　　　　　　　　　　　　　　　　　　　　　　　　　CIP

First Pocket Books trade paperback printing July 1999

10　9　8　7　6　5　4　3　2　1

POCKET and colophon are registered trademarks of Simon & Schuster Inc.

Designed by Helene Berinsky
Cover design by Tom McKeveny

Printed in the U.S.A.

This book is dedicated to Abe Herman
on his ninetieth birthday
for his wit and wisdom and for
infecting his son with a love of learning.

Acknowledgments

I deeply appreciate the kindness and encouragement of my former students, Professors Ernie Lepore of Rutgers University and Lynn Pasquerella of the University of Rhode Island, who read this bizarre and sometimes unphilosophic manuscript diligently and with good grace. Their suggestions were invaluable. I would have liked to blame them for my errors and inanities, but I have to acknowledge (since this is an acknowledgment) that the flaws are without exception mine. I also want to thank my wife Dr. Gail Neary Herman for her patience and careful reading of the MS, my daughter Leta for her astute editorial commentary, and Jeffrey Tomcsik, a recent graduate of an undergraduate philosophy department, who gave me a youth perspective I once-upon-a-time had but now lack and cannot recall.

—S.H.

Contents

PHILOSOPHY

Our planet abounds with philosophers, or so it seems. To some people, Yogi Berra's a philosopher: "It ain't over till it's over" is pretty metaphysical, at least for the Bronx. The guy next door is stoical about his dog's defecatory habits ("Sh——t happens," he says, shrugging), and his kids are natural-born epistemologists ("Don't tell me how to lead my life, Pops; you can't know what's best for me"). In a world full of philosophizers, you'd think we'd all know by now what philosophy is and what it is not. Guess what? We don't.

In fact, most of us don't even know how to ask a decent philosophical question, even when it comes from some deep and personal bout of feverish introspection.

For example, for most of us there's only one big-deal question we have about the atmospherics of existence. It's this:

WHAT IS THE MEANING OF LIFE?

Good question, right? Wrong. Because any answer you get—from "compulsive reproduction" to "a perfect backstroke"—is likely to be "philosophical," but only if your meaning of *philosophy* is interchangeable with your meaning of *whimsy*. The truth is, we not only don't know what philosophy is, we don't even have a sure sense of

WHAT PHILOSOPHY ISN'T

- **Philosophy isn't science**, although science had its origins in philosophy, and many philosophers have been scientifically minded. Experimentation is essential to the scientific enterprise, and both physical and behavioral scientists experiment. Philosophy is classified as a humanity, and if you're lucky, you may someday parlay your reading of this volume of the *Pocket Professor* into humanities credits at some unsuspecting or lax university. Unlike scientists, philosophers don't experiment. To do so would be to risk their cushy status as humanists. Some renegades have had dual careers and made major contributions to the special sciences, but once they wash the beakers, turn off the current, and exchange their lab coats for their philosophic hats, they stop experimenting. So what do philosophers do? Mostly they think and occasionally they communicate their thoughts to other philosophers, who on occasion interrupt their thoughts to listen to them. Being thoughtful in this way is not the same as being agreeable, however. Philosophers often split up into camps and behave in the most unthoughtful and disagreeable manner, much like Republicans and Democrats. A philosophy conference can be a hoot, though, at least as entertaining as the Friday-night fights—but more expensive.

- **Philosophy isn't art.** Artists produce aesthetic objects that often occasion aesthetic experiences in the viewer. Philosophers can be creative and imaginative, too, but what they produce is typically anaesthetic, works so ponderous and dreary that they have been known to turn incurable insomniacs into Rip Van Winkles. The philosopher's primary interest is not beauty but truth. John Keats, the English Romantic poet, disputed the distinction, claiming in his "Ode on a Grecian Urn" that "beauty is truth, truth beauty," a sentiment you may find aesthetically appealing. Many an unromantic philosopher will tell you this is false. The only sorts of things that can be true are statements. Beauty may grace a Grecian urn, but it's not the sort of thing that can be true. More on this later.

- **Philosophy isn't religion**, either, although the subject matter of the two disciplines sometimes overlaps, and the development of the two sometimes got intertwined in a way that makes disentangling them difficult. The main difference is the basis for belief. For example, both disciplines have wondered whether God exists. Philosophers have a neat word: *qua* (pronounced "quay"). The term is Latin, and it means "in the capacity of." Theologians *qua* theologians—that is, in their capacity as theologians—have relied primarily on *revelation* and *authority* as bases for religious belief; philosophers have a long history of questioning both. Some philosophers and even some theologians *qua* philosophers have offered proofs of God's existence as an alternative basis for religious belief.

There's a lot more that we can say is not philosophy. On the street, *philosophy* is often used very loosely to refer to a wide spectrum of opinions and theories. "What's your philosophy on the rising price of cabbage?" "What's your philosophy on natural childbirth?" "What's your philosophy on hitting a curve ball to right field?" This everyday way of understanding philosophy practically cuts the heart out of the discipline.

Book publishers have added to the confusion. Among the trendy set, philosophy is often associated with heavy thinking. Being philosophical (even nerdy) can be chic (witness Woody Allen). In upscale bookstores, you can plummet the depths of the deepest deep, all the while urbanely sipping a down-to-earth robust double espresso.

Here's our top 10 picks for a pseudophilosophy Pulitzer:

TEN REASONS WHY *PHILOSOPHY* IS ONE OF THE MOST MISUSED WORDS IN THE ENGLISH LANGUAGE

1. *The Celestine Prophecy: An Adventure,* by James Redfield
2. *The Tao of Pooh,* by Benjamin Hoff
3. *Going for Broke; My Philosophy of Winning Golf,* by Arnold Palmer, with William Barry Furlong
4. *The Official Rules of Life: For Those of You Who Thought You'd Mastered Life's Little Instructions and Learned Everything You Needed to Know,* by Seth Godin
5. *Life's Little Instruction Book,* by H. Jackson Brown Jr.
6. *All I Really Need to Know I Learned in Kindergarten: Uncommon Thoughts on Common Things,* by Robert Fulghum
7. *Illusions: The Adventures of a Reluctant Messiah,* by Richard Bach
8. *Everything I Know I Learned on Acid,* by Coco Pekelis
9. *The Book of Virtues: A Treasury of Great Moral Stories,* edited by William J. Bennett
10. Any Ayn Rand novel or any book about the Zen of anything

Hints of the philosophical now appear in book titles with about the same frequency that the term *natural* appears on cereal boxes. Not everything that's labeled *philosophy* is.

EST? NON-EST? THE FALLEN EMPIRE
OF WERNER ERHARD

The last time we saw him, the founder of the movement est (Erhard seminar training), Werner Erhard, was on TV. He was on the lam from the law and doing a satellite remote from somewhere in deep, dark Russia. In one short hour on a news channel, Erhard tried to explain how one of the networks had come to do an earlier exposé on him. His sins, according to the pursuing news crew and the people they had interviewed, ranged from income tax evasion to sexual abuse to telling his est followers that he was a god.

If you caught the broadcast, you would have seen Erhard blaming all his legal and family troubles on rival guru L. Ron Hubbard and his Scientology followers. He groused about a conspiracy, a plot to get him, and told viewers he was running for his life. All this from the man who made terms like *responsibility* and *integrity* household words during the 1970s and 1980s when he held in thrall auditoriums filled with people who would rather listen to Werner than take a leak. (He forbade the use of toilets during his endless tirades.)

ARGUMENTUM AD HOMINEM

The above sarcasm leveled at Werner illustrates an informal logical fallacy. In English, *argumentum ad hominem* means "argument against character rather than precepts." One attacks the person—in this case, his character and circumstances—rather than his viewpoints. Philosophers are trained to avoid such informal fallacies, as delicious as they sometimes are. Social or sexual deviance is no guarantee that a perp (TV cop lingo for a perpetrator) is not speaking the truth. However much of a slug Werner is or is not, he can assert the truth from time to time just like you. For all we know, he might be a god.

We might, of course, question his claim as well as the benevolence and omnipotence of his deity. On our personal Richter scale, flight to Russia doesn't exactly qualify as even a minor miracle. One would think that a god would have skipped to a more commodious clime, say Buenos Aires or Mount Olympus or at the minimum the backwoods of Montana where like the Unabomber one could publish long and tedious treatises and still elude his pursuers for 15 years or so. (For more on informal fallacies, see below.)

L. RON HUBBARD'S THEFT-PROOF TEXTBOOK:
DYING FOR *DIANETICS*

Tom Cruise, John Travolta, Kirstie Alley, Isaac Hayes, and Lisa Marie Presley have all claimed to be true L. Ron believers. Apparently the petty thieves who roam the streets of New York City are not. We say this on the basis of our own set of observations. As even casual visitors know, in Manhattan it is never wise to set something down on the sidewalk, not even for a moment, unless you never want to see it again. The exception to this rule, of course, is L. Ron Hubbard's book *Dianetics: The Modern Science of Mental Health.*

For years, one of this book's authors lived down the street from the New York headquarters of the Church of Scientology and would marvel at how the faithful could leave a table full of copies of *Dianetics* on the sidewalk for anyone to take. In fact, they encouraged purloining the text. Yet not a one would ever disappear. The conclusion one might draw? When it comes to philosophy, thieves in New York City are like big old wily lunkers cruising a lake for prey. They can tell the difference between a lure and the genuine article.

PHILOSOPHY'S POP SUBCONTRACTOR:
MARIANNE WILLIAMSON

The story of Marianne Williamson reminds us of the old playground game Telephone. In this case, the game started in the ear of New York City psychologist Helen Schucman when one day out of the blue a voice in the air spoke to her and said, "This is a course in miracles; please take notes." Seven years later, the voice stopped dictating and Helen set down her pen, having written a 1,255-page book called *A Course in Miracles* based on the teachings of the voice.

At about the same time that Helen Schucman was taking dictation from God, young Marianne Williamson was using a lot of drugs, failing as a jazz singer, and jumping in and out of relationships. In her own words, she was a "total mess." A mess, that is, until she picked up a copy of *A Course in Miracles* lying on a friend's coffee table. (Do you detect another mean-spirited *argumentum ad hominem* brewing up here?)

Here's where the story gets really interesting: Marianne read Helen's book and immediately straightened up her life. She then started speaking to others about *A Course in Miracles,* first in small groups and then to large auditoriums, and eventually wound up making scads of money traveling around the world giving speeches and seminars and writing a best-seller based on her reflections on the principles the voice had whispered into Helen's ear.

Whatever philosophy is, you can pretty well bet it isn't what Helen and Marianne dish up for popular consumption. Hearing voices is as much evidence for madness as for revelation. But giving them the benefit of the doubt, they are at best authors in religious studies. When it comes to Werner and Ron L., it's harder to say. Pseudophilosophy and bad philosophy are different. Werner's and L. Ron's works drip with scientific terminology, although their theories are not science. Maybe they are philosophizing after all, just badly.

INFINITE PROPOSITIONS

When you explain something by stating what it is not, you have cleared away one possibility yet come no closer to clarifying what that thing is. Immanuel Kant, a philosopher whom we will meet later, referred to such negative assertions as infinite propositions. For example: "Philosophy is not biology"; "Philosophy is not made of green cheese"; "Philosophy is not vegetable or mineral"; "Philosophy is not red." You can go on this way indefinitely without ever explaining what philosophy is. Unless your motivation is to have a little fun along the way (as ours is), starting a philosophy text using this negative approach is not very fruitful. So let's get on with what the discipline is.

PHILOSOPHY: WHAT IT IS

In the original Greek, the term *philosophy* meant "the study, pursuit, or love of wisdom." Originally philosophy included various disciplines we today think of as natural or behavioral sciences. In the past, physical scientists were not even called scientists; they were considered philosophers and, accordingly, bore the name *natural philosophers.* This terminology may seem surprising until one reflects on the fact that before the seventeenth century inquiry was rarely experimental. Mostly, investigations were speculative, as philosophy remains for the most part today. But as the different disciplines specialized in their investigations of nature (biology, chemistry, physics, and astronomy) and later the human experience (psychology, anthropology, and sociology), the special sciences emerged in their own right, and the domain of philosophy shrunk to what it is today.

According to tradition, philosophy has five main branches: metaphysics, epistemology, ethics, aesthetics, and logic. The unifying feature among all the branches is their methodology. Regardless of the branch, *reason* is the philosopher's primary tool of inquiry. Yet philosophers, especially with the advance of science since the sixteenth century, have increasingly tended to treat science with respect, incorporating relevant findings into their own theories and eschewing positions that contradict scientific belief (see Three Methods of Philosophic Analysis, page 28).

WHAT PROFESSIONAL PHILOSOPHERS TALK ABOUT WHEN THEY PHILOSOPHIZE

What kind of club is this? What do you have to do to join? Without giving away any philosophers' club secrets or rites, we can divulge that you will acquire a nickname of sorts if selected: metaphysician, epistemologist, ethicist, aesthetician, logician, or the like (depending on the area of philosophy in which you specialize).

FIVE MAIN BRANCHES OF PHILOSOPHY

Each branch has a scope of inquiry, each raising its own questions.

METAPHYSICS

You learned about atomic theory in school, and you probably believe that atoms and subatomic particles make up the material world you inhabit. Is everything entirely made up of matter? What about human beings? What is the status of minds or souls? Do they belong to the same order of reality as physical objects, or do they belong to a different order of reality? What about your experience? According to atomic theory, atoms are colorless, odorless, and tasteless particles swirling about in space. Yet the oranges you buy in the supermarket are orange and smell and taste sweet. Is your experience of the orange mistaken? Is there a difference between the way the world is and the way it appears to you?

EPISTEMOLOGY

In 1491, did Europeans *know* that the world was flat? Do we *know* today that it is not? What is knowledge? What is the relationship of knowledge to belief or opinion? What is the relationship between the person who knows something and the thing known? What are the types and sources of knowledge? How do people acquire knowledge? Are there limits to what the human mind can know? What counts as a rational justification for a belief you hold? Is Helen Schucman's hearing voices a rational basis for her beliefs?

ETHICS

If a woman chooses to abort her fetus, is her action *right or wrong?* Is she a *good or bad* person? Are there principles that can guide our moral judgment on this and other life decisions we confront? The Bible offers one set of principles. But are the Ten Commandments absolute? Are there circumstances in which killing is permissible or justified or right? What true principles, if any, justify making exceptions for, say, capital punishment, war, or self-defense?

AESTHETICS

What is an art object? What determines whether a work of art is good? What is a creative act? What is aesthetic experience? Is liking a work of art the same as judging it good?

LOGIC

What is good reasoning? Are there ways to find out with certainty whether reasoning is good? Can rules of thought be developed and systemized as guides to good reasoning?

If you want to travel in any of these philosophic disciplines, the chances are that you are going to need a road map. Here are some useful directions.

THE BASICS, PHILOSOPHICALLY SPEAKING

METAPHYSICS

Ironically, this field of study bears the name *metaphysics* more as a happy accident and matter of coincidence. As the story goes, when Aristotle finished writing a book on this previously unnamed subject, he named his work *Metaphysics* because it happened to follow after (that is, *meta*) the book he had written on physics. However, the coincidence is instructive because metaphysicians study reality at a more general level than even physicists do. Instead of studying particular types of being, such as atoms, stars, light, electricity, or magnetism, metaphysicians, according to tradition, study being in general.

Let's call anything that exists an existent. Consider your best buddies Alphonse, Henrietta, and Egbert. Each is different, but they all belong to general classes. They are friends of yours, and even more generally, they are citizens of the United States, and even more generally still, they are people. You probably believe that there is a huge list of other types of existents, including, rocks, rock stars, trees, moose, mice, melons, and machines. All these, along with Alphonse, Henrietta, and Egbert, belong to a general class, too. They are all material objects. The metaphysician in you might conclude that matter is a type of being in general.

With your metaphysical curiosity now aroused, you might also wonder whether matter is the only type of being in general. Does, for example, God, an immaterial being, exist? What about you? Is your mind nothing more than a hunk of gray matter? Are human beings merely highly organized units of physical reality, advanced robots, but with flesh, sinews, and muscles instead of wire, cogs, and electronic circuitry? In addition, you might wonder about the nature of matter, whether it has any properties, and what the relationship of matter is to the properties it has.

Congratulations! You are well on your way to becoming a metaphysician, which regrettably does not imply that you are a physician, so you can abandon all hope that you can ever cure yourself of the metaphysical bug that is this very minute diving into your cerebral arteries. You may never think like a normal person again.

> If your metaphysical infection turns out to be severe enough, you will soon be ready for the most advanced form of philosophic bubbleheadedness. Students of French literature may be reminded of Alfred (*Ubu roi*) Jarry and the fin-de-siècle school of French "pataphysics." When asked what pataphysics was, Jarry replied that pataphysics is to metaphysics what metaphysics is to physics. (For more, see Roger Shattuck's *Banquet Years: The Arts in France, 1885–1918,* a collection of profiles of Jarry, Eric Satie, Henri Rousseau, and other artistic bad boys in France, c. 1900.)

EPISTEMOLOGY

Michael Feldman of National Public Radio fame starts each one of his weekly shows with the epistemological question "Well, whad'ya know?" His audience of hardy Wisconsinites enthusiastically replies, "Nothing. What about you?" For the moment these cheeseheads have become willing and enthusiastic, albeit for the most part innocent, epistemologists.

Epistemology is the theory of knowledge. The term derives from the Greek term *episteme,* which means "to know." Knowledge and a theory of knowledge are not identical. You might know that $2 + 2 = 4$. Epistemologists have theorized about whether this mathematical truth is knowledge and about whether it is the same type of knowledge as the knowledge you have when you acknowledge that the print on this page is black. Epistemologists have also theorized about how you come to acquire such knowledge. There are two main schools of thought on the subject:

- Empiricists think we get our knowledge *a posteriori,* or from experience. One notable father of empiricism was John Locke, who believed that the human mind is born a tabula rasa, or blank slate, which we fill in as our life experience unfolds. Unwittingly, most people are empiricists. For them "seeing (that is, sensing) is believing." They're Harry Truman's kind of folk. "I'm from Missouri. You gotta *show* me!"
- Rationalists, on the other hand, think we get our knowledge *a priori,* implanted in the mind at birth or before or, more generally, independently of experience. Plato was a father of the rationalist tradition. He believed that all knowledge is acquired before we are born. At birth, this knowledge is transferred into our subconscious minds. According to Plato, learning becomes a process of remembering the innate knowledge already stored within us.

As part of a long tradition, epistemologists distinguish knowledge and belief. According to this tradition, beliefs can be mistaken; knowledge cannot. A twist on this point is that you can also be mistaken in your belief that you have knowledge. A lot of folks once thought they knew that the earth was flat. But they were wrong to believe that they had such knowledge.

Note that epistemology and metaphysics are often related disciplines. An epistemologist might theorize about whether fundamental reality could be known, for example.

ETHICS

"Should I or shouldn't I?" The behavioral sciences and ethics have a common feature: They are both concerned with issues related to human conduct. But this resemblance is superficial. Behavioral scientists study how human beings do behave under varying conditions, and they try to discern lawful patterns of conduct. Ethicists, on the other hand, are concerned not with how people do in fact behave but with how they ought or ought not to behave. They are concerned with duty and obligation, right and wrong conduct, and good and bad intentions.

Ethics is said to be a normative science because it examines and sometimes seeks to establish norms or standards of conduct. Let's say you see a neighbor being thrashed by six burly trucker, longshoreman, pro lineman types and you haven't yet finished your Charles Atlas course or had the opportunity to be the grasshopper to some kung fu master—plus you are in a very isolated spot and cannot call the police or secure some other form of help. Under these circumstances, are you obligated to come to your neighbor's aid even though the odds are statistically just about a sure bet that if you did help, you'd get your butt kicked, and for all that trouble, you're not going to save your neighbor's bacon anyhow? What's the right thing to do?

Note that ethics and epistemology can also be related. For example, philosophers have wondered whether it is possible to know with certainty what is good. Ethics can also give rise to metaphysical questions: Is a person good in the same sense that she is tall? Most people think that tallness is a property some people possess. Is goodness a property in the same way? Or does goodness belong to another order of reality?

AESTHETICS

Aesthetics is the philosophy of art. What is genuine art? Is industrial music art or noise? Does Barry Manilow rank up there with those all-star Hall of Famers Bach, Mozart, and Beethoven? What about the Spice Girls or Nine Inch Nails? Or for that matter, what about you when you happen to hum up some jaunty little ditty in the shower? Is "I'm a Little Teapot" art?

In the visual arts, does all good art have to imitate peaches, apples, lemons, Christ, saints, woodland scenes, Sabine women, cherubim, or the like? Or can one create abstract art like Pablo Picasso did, building figures out of triangles, cubes, and cylinders, sometimes putting heads, arms, and other bodily parts in the most surprising and on occasion unseemly places, sometimes making people look like precursors of Robocop? And what about Jackson Pollock, who dripped paint from cans onto canvas on the floor beneath him and lived to see his works immortalized in New York's Museum of Modern Art, right up there on the walls with such luminaries as Claude Monet? Is Pollock's work in any significant way different from the smear jobs of two-year-olds or aesthetically minded chimpanzees? (Or maybe their artwork is just as valid and should be hung in galleries alongside Pollock's.)

Traditionally, aesthetics focused on what came to be called the aesthetics triad:

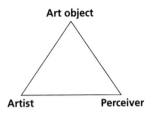

The artist creates the art object that the perceivers experience and sometimes judge. Respectively, artists and perceivers can have creative and aesthetic experiences that some believe are special psychological states different from those experienced in ordinary life. Artists and perceivers can also render aesthetic judgments, aesthetically valuing or devaluing art objects (and possibly other objects as well), judging them to be beautiful, ugly, sublime, good, bad, neutral or the like.

As with ethics, aesthetics is normative. In other words, aestheticians have endeavored to identify standards or norms for determining whether objects are works of art or just junk, whether acts are creative or just stupid, and whether art objects are good or beautiful or bad-ugly. Can ugly artwork still be good art?

LOGIC

Logic is the study of good reasoning. The main task of the logician is to devise or discover procedures, rules, and standards by which to guide and judge reasoning or inference. Although there are several types of reasoning or inference, the type that will concern us here is called deduction. Deductive reasoning is good or bad, or, as philosophers say, valid or invalid. To determine the validity or invalidity of reasoning, logicians study arguments. For logicians, the term *argument* has a technical sense. An argument is a group of statements, one of which is the conclusion and the remaining ones are the premises or the reasons advanced in favor of the conclusion. An argument is valid provided that it is impossible for its premises to be true yet its conclusion false.

Consider this example: All dogs are mammals. Lassie is a dog. So Lassie is a mammal. This argument is good—that is, valid—because the conclusion "Lassie is a mammal" follows deductively from the premises. If the premises are true (as they happen to be in this instance), then the conclusion *must* be true as well. Now consider this argument: All dogs are fish. Lassie is a dog. So Lassie is a fish. You might be surprised to learn that this argument is also valid because it is impossible for the premises to be true yet the conclusion false. Although the first premise and the conclusion are as a matter of fact false, ask yourself what would happen if the first premise were true.

Then it would be impossible for the conclusion to be false. So the argument satisfies the formal definition of *validity*. A false conclusion can deductively follow from false premises.

Arguments are deductively valid based on their logical form, and it so happens that the two arguments presented above have the same logical form:

All _____ are _____.
X is a _____.
So X is a _____.

The line, the dashes, and the X are placeholders like the letters x, y, and z in an algebraic formula. Read this argument form as follows: All lines are dashes. X is a line. So X is a dash. Any trio of statements that fits this logical form or pattern results in a deductively valid argument regardless of the content you plug into the lines—X's and dashes—that is, the placeholders.

Logicians have rules. To ensure that your reasoning is valid and to avoid offending the gods of reason who are not above indulging in paroxysms of punitive irrationality from time to time, obey the rules!

Philosophy: Does It Matter?

As the title of that old time favorite song says, "It All Depends on You." Lots of people live their lives perfectly well without ever becoming philosophical, at least beyond the occasional "Oh, well." One strand of classical Greek thought stands solidly in their corner. "Ignorance," as people say, "is bliss." A corollary is that too much knowledge is a dangerous thing.

But whether it is wise or beneficial to become philosophical is in many cases irrelevant. If you tailgate some philosopher's recreational 4 × 4 closely enough, you might read this less than classical bumper sticker: "Philosophy happens"—at least it does to some people.

Imagine a day like any other. You are by nature a common sense, down-to-earth sort. By no means would you consider yourself "deep," and you did not have the slightest hint that you would on this day find yourself immersed in philosophical perplexity. Yet you've just finished the latest in a seemingly never-ending series of quarterly reports and poured your fifth cup of coffee (which may account for the strange events about to happen) when the idle thought "Wonder if I should change careers?" flits across your unsuspecting mind like a subliminal department-store message urging you to buy Hula Hoops *now*. Before you know it, other more philosophic questions whisk into your consciousness, and in the blink of your mind's eye you've dropped off the square edge of the earth into that vapory realm we call philosophy. You ask yourself

What the hell am I doing this for? Is this all there is to life? Is this what life is all about? *"What the hell is the meaning of life, anyway?"*

WHY BIG QUESTIONS HURT

Even pausing for a moment to consider a question about the worth or meaning of one's own existence is often enough to precipitate migraine headaches equal to a head blow by a large skillet. Amazingly, advertisers for aspirin brands, sedatives, and lethal poisons haven't yet discovered the potential of such questions for driving scads of people into a grand brain-pounding funk. By the way, if you're one of those poor benighted devils whom fate has singled out for special susceptibility to such intellectual maladies, make haste to your nearest doctor of philosophy, at least one of whom would tell you that one of the best antidotes for chronic philosophic angst is humor and that the best prescription is to take at least one joke daily. We might as well laugh; it beats the alternative.

But why are these questions so perplexing? For one thing, a lot of us think that every one-sentence question has a one-sentence answer: "The meaning of life is plums" would be nice. But answers to philosophic questions are almost never so simple. Contemplating the meaning of life can be like a bad day fishing with a Cub Scout troop of five-year-olds. The kids keep twitching and whining and pestering you about when they're going to catch the big fish. After what seems like an eternity of baiting and untangling lines, you gleefully help one of the little twerps reel in a six-inch perch, whereupon the scouts, who think unity a virtue, begin altogether to kvetch and clamor about wanting to catch the *big* fish. Modest progress is just not good enough for the little ingrates. And so it is with the meaning of life. People tend to want the whole enchilada.

If you happen to have the pluck to consult the great philosophers about your jumbo question regarding the meaning of life,
there's a good chance you'll get more than you bargained for. Questions that appear simple to the unphilosophic eye often turn out to
be complex to the trained eye of the philosopher, who sees questions with the magnifying intensity of an electron microscope. For
the philosopher, really *big* and very complex questions often lie hidden within the seeming simplicity of other ones. For example:

What Do You Mean by *Life*?

When people ask about the meaning of life, mostly what they
care about is human life. We humans don't usually get that lit up
over the meaning of a rabbit's, dog's, or plum's life (although sometimes we do). But for the sake of getting started, let's stick with
human life and presume that we know it, pretty roughly, when we
see it.

The Meaning of Life?

When we ask, "What is *the* meaning of life?" our question contains what philosophers call a definite description. Typically, definite descriptions begin with the article *the,* and they perform a
particular function in language. If, for example, we say, "The loudest dog has fleas," we are asserting that a loudest dog exists, that
only one loudest dog exists, and that *that* is the dog with fleas. In
the case of our big question, the use of the definite description
implies that there is a meaning of life and that there is one—and
only one—meaning of life.

If you want to be a philosopher, you have to pack light. You
don't want to carry sets of assumptions around with you all day.
Among other things, lousy assumptions make your day-to-day life
harder than it no doubt already is. For example, let's say you're a
cop. In fact, just for the entertainment value of it all, let's say you're
Columbo, the wrinkled, trench-coated forensic cogitator on TV. A
corpse was found lying on the pavement, having fallen from a
rooftop. Columbo could have put the inevitable whodunit question
in the form of a definite description: "Duh, I wonder who *the* murderer is?" Then like an errant knight, he would have lit out, his feet
getting flatter by the minute, on a wild goose chase, pushing his

tired 1963 Puttmobile beyond its limits, all because he framed his question in a way that failed to take account of two other possibilities: The guy wasn't murdered at all (he tripped and fell), or he was murdered, but three (not one) dastardly felons did it. Functioning with mafioso-like precision, the three villains had chucked the poor bugger off the roof.

If our man asks the right questions in the right order and spares himself the unsavory consequences of the ambiguities of language, he'll do just fine. "Was a murder committed?" he asks first. And if so, was there one or more than one murderer?

Philosophers are detectives of a sort. Like Columbo, they frame their questions carefully. Instead of asking about *the* meaning of life, a skillful philosopher would ask first whether life has any meaning at all, and, if so, whether it has one or more than one meaning.

What's the Meaning of *Meaning*?

Not to sound Clintonian here, but ironically, the meaning of *meaning* is ambiguous. *Meaning* sometimes pertains to language. We ask for the meaning of words. In response, we often offer definitions. But when we ask about the meaning of life, we are typically not asking what the word *life* means. Rather, we are asking about the significance of human existence. However, using the term *significance* does nothing to clarify our understanding, since *significance* is ambiguous in the very same way that *meaning* is. Sometimes we want to know the signification of a word. We want to know its meaning. But when people ask your opinion about the significance of life, the odds are that what they really want to know is whether life has purpose or value.

So our giant question becomes "Does life have purpose or value?" This question is really two questions in one:

- Does life have purpose?

and

- Does life have value?

Presumably, something like a sunset might have value without having a purpose. So let's keep these questions disentangled in our minds.

If someone asks you why you are standing on one foot with your tongue hanging out limply to the left side of your mouth and your right pinky on the tip of your nose, and you answer, "No reason," then your act seems senseless and pointless. But if you answer that you are rehearsing for a part as a clown, then your action becomes intelligible and makes sense. It takes on meaning or significance in the sense that your action was undertaken for a *purpose*. Stating your purpose is giving a *reason* for your action. It explains your behavior to an extent.

Your purpose, one might argue, also confers value on your action. Presumably, you want to play the part of the clown because you value playing the role. Your rehearsing is a means to an end. Since the end or purpose has value, it confers value on the means—the rehearsing—used to attain it.

Does life then have meaning in the sense that it has purpose or value? Before attempting an answer, we should clarify what we mean by *purpose* and *value,* but you're probably sick of this whole business by now, so we'll just assume that you know what purpose and value are, and we'll carry on from there.

WHERE DOES THIS LEAVE US?

We need to answer the questions Does human life have purpose? and Does it have value? These questions might seem pretty nutty. After all, why would anyone think that human life doesn't have purpose or value? People have all kinds of values and purposes, not the least of which is life itself and working hard to preserve it, even under the most wretched circumstances.

Let's not jump too hastily to conclusions, though. The language we are

ANALYTIC PHILOSOPHY

You have just had a little demonstration of analytic philosophy at work. Analytic philosophers belong to a contemporary philosophic school, which became influential first in England and the United States but now has adherents in continental Europe and elsewhere. This brand of philosophy is called analytic because it seeks to answer philosophic questions using analysis—a process of breaking complex issues into simpler parts. Our analysis began with an attempt to clarify what is meant by *life.* Then we examined the definite description *the meaning of life,* and we made explicit the assumptions to which the use of the term *the* committed us. Next we clarified the meaning of *meaning* as used in the question. Through this process, we were able to clarify the question and avoid, to an extent, unwarranted assumptions before attempting an answer.

A DIGRESSION . . . OR, GLOOM, DOOM, AND PESSIMISM: GENESIS ACCORDING TO THE GOSPEL OF SCIENCE

In the beginning, the universe was a teeny weeny smidgen of highly compressed matter, much much smaller than a pea. To get the idea, imagine a New York City subway car in the worst rush hour ever. Imagine, too, some diabolical transit company wise guys using a hydraulic ramrod to squeeze a billion more people into the already cramped space. Next, send the train careening north from 42nd to 59th Streets, everyone aboard starving for the air forced out of their compressed and flattened lungs. At last the train screeches to a stop, its doors part, and the people hurl outward with magnum supergun force and violence as oxygen-starved lungs inhale the sweet familiar fragrance of the New York City underground.

This is kind of the way the universe began, according to many contemporary scientists. The true geologic calendar commenced on the equivalent of the Fourth of July, 0000, with a *big bang.* Heavenly bodies, gases, dust, fire, and brimstone were propelled outward at extremely high velocity and are even to this day expanding outward from the central explosion.

In the frigid cold of space, fireballs cooled and gases condensed and in instances liquefied. Gravity turned some of the speeding bodies from their straight-line projectory to the end of the universe until these bodies circumscribed the planetary orbits of solar systems. In one remote corner of the universe, the one we call home, elemental particles making up the liquid and gases of the earth swirled and collided according to Newton's laws of mechanics, just like so many bumper cars at Coney Island, forming one chemical mix and then another until amino acids, the building blocks of life, developed. Then the sun radiated the goo to just the right degree, and a microscopic single-celled creature formed, came to life, divided, and multiplied.

But the earth's first tenants hadn't celebrated more than a fortnight before they began a never-ending struggle to survive in a stingy and begrudging world, living thing pitted against living thing unto death. Those with traits best suited to survival in the circumstances of their environment lived to procreate and perpetuate their favorable traits. The laws of genetics also intervened, determining occasional mutations, which on rare occasion were better suited to their environments than their progenitors. Through these means species varied and diversification of the kingdom of life became increasingly complex and organized until an amphibian walked out of the primordial ooze and established life on terra firma. Once legs evolved, it was a hop, skip, a swing or two from branch to branch, and a jump before the upper primates evolved into human beings. So that's the story of how we came to be and why it is that princes and princesses still have an uncontrollable urge to kiss frogs. (But does it explain Marilyn Manson?)

What does the history of creation from the first pop to the most recent fizz have to tell us about the big question? Does life have purpose or value, or doesn't it? According to one scientific world view, the whole development of human life from the Fourth of July, 0000, to now has been the product of bits and hunks of matter interacting according to mechanical laws that describe the universe, which is fundamentally purposeless and without value. The universe just is. According to another, apparently random developments actually seem to fall into a pattern that ultimately adheres to a cosmic design. In other words, shit happens.

But what about us, you ask? We have purposes, and we have values. True 'nough. You may value your life and the lives of your families and friends, and you may even value life itself. But your valuing life doesn't necessarily make it actually valuable, any more than your admiring mayhem makes it admirable. Or, your valuing life may have nothing to do with *your* purposes but may well have to do with some other set of purposes, all of which may perhaps be unknowable. You may be a pawn on someone else's chessboard.

Science project: Australian physicist Paul Davies is one of a growing number of scientists finding less and less that is random about the universe. A good introduction: Davies's *Mind of God: The Scientific Basis for a Rational World.*

using here is ambiguous and needs to be clarified first. In one sense, whatever is valued is valuable. Don't believe that? Go to an auction and see for yourself. If you value life, for example, then life is certainly valuable *in the sense* that it *can be* valued. However, it doesn't follow that life is valuable *in the sense* that it *has* value or worth. If you value life, you may be valuing something inherently valueless.

As to our purposes, they all come to nought. Your great-great-great-great-grandmother died perhaps sometime in the early to mid-nineteenth century, not all that long ago. Until relatively recently, few people knew the name of their esteemed ancestors six times removed or where they lived or lay buried. In fact, see how well you can do just naming all of your great-grandparents. Yet your great-great-great-great grandmother had dreams, goals, and purposes just like you, but they were *hers,* and in the larger scheme of things, they have proved vainglorious. Who knows or remembers what she desired or strove for, what mattered to her, or what she cared about? She and her purposes are utterly lost, extinguished, obliterated. And so it will be with you and everyone else *except* the *Pocket Professor's* authors, who exercise the power of the pen in their own vainglorious attempt to exempt themselves from such a dismal end.

OBSOLETE OZYMANDIAS

You may remember Percy Bysshe Shelley's poem "Ozymandias." Ozymandias was a great and feared king of old who erected as a monument to himself a massive and forbidding statue. Now it lies in ruins in the middle of a vast and empty dessert with not a human soul to see or contemplate it. Yet there on its pedestal inscribed for no eyes to read are the words

> My name is Ozymandias,
>   King of Kings,
> Look on my Works, ye Mighty,
>   and despair!

So it is with all of us. All our purposes, all our struggles, all our works come to nothing in the long run. From dust to dust—or as in the case of Ozymandias, from silica to silica.

Speaking for himself, presumably— but assuming everyone cared— philosopher Bertrand Russell once offered a skeptical account regarding the purposeless of existence. See his *Why I Am Not a Christian.*

To this pessimistic estimate of our posterity, one might reply that purpose transcends the life and aspirations of any one individual or species. Even if the authors' lives or each individual life comes to nought in the long run, even if the entire human race and all purposes are extinguished from the universe for a time, purpose will still have existed as part of history and through evolution will make its appearance again in the course of time. But these new purposes will be the purposes of beings who inhabit the universe, perhaps of what they wanted to accomplish in their lives or what they hoped their offspring or others might accomplish in theirs. But could any of these individuals establish a purpose for life itself? Or is life inherently purposeless?

THREE VIEWS ON WHETHER LIFE HAS MEANING

THE GOSPEL ACCORDING TO THE GOSPEL

In the beginning, God created the universe *ex nihilo,* out of nothing, in a spectacular demonstration of mind over emptiness and matter. The creation included human life in the persons of Adam and Eve, who willfully flounted God's will, did the deed, and spawned the population explosion that is responsible for the imperfect human life forms crawling all over the planet today.

The human being is a composite of body and soul. Soul is spirit, a type of reality that is outside the domain of scientific inquiry. Here's a nice morsel of metaphysics for you: God, too, is a spirit, one who exists outside the universe and is its creator. God is a perfect being: omnipotent (all powerful), omniscient (all knowing), and omnibenevolent (all good).

The Plan

God created the universe according to a divine plan. Everything, including human beings, has a purpose in this plan. We're not all in agreement on what the plan is, exactly, but one version goes like this: A main—if not *the*—purpose of life is aviational, so to speak—to earn one's wings. Life is God's test to see who is worthy of the kingdom of heaven. Although we are being tested our whole lives long, the Scoring Division of the Holy Sepulcher won't announce the final results until we have departed this mortal coil. In brief, the ultimate purpose of life is to pass, yet many American students will be dismayed to learn that it's impossible to cheat. Other interpreters of this gospel think that God has a purpose in mind for us but that that purpose is beyond the ability of human minds to fathom, at least in this life. Either way, life does have a purpose and it does have value. God, whose existence is *outside* the physical realm, is in a position to give the totality of human life a purpose because God can use human life for His (or Her? or Its?) own ends. Life then becomes a means to God's purposes for it.

> **IT'S THE BEST A RATIONAL GOD COULD DO**
>
> Gottfried Wilhelm Leibniz (1646–1716) was lampooned in Voltaire's (1694–1778) *Candide*. According to Leibniz, God chose the best of all possible worlds for human beings from an infinite array of possible rational designs. Creating a world according to Newton's natural laws of mechanics was God's way of creating the combination of the greatest variety and the greatest order. In *Candide,* the philosopher Dr. Pangloss (who manages to put a high-gloss shine on every disaster) counsels the young hero Candide that this is the best of all possible worlds, but the hapless Candide experiences one grave misfortune after another until at the end, he has had enough of philosophy and stays home out of harm's way, quietly cultivating his own garden.

Life Also Has Value

As the product of God's perfection, creation is perfect, too, although it may not always seem so to lowly mortal intellects like ours. Creation couldn't be perfect yet lack value, indeed infinite value. So life, according to the gospel according to the gospel, has both purpose and value.

GOD'S UNDERTAKER

For an irreverent counterpart to Christ's Sermon on the Mount, read Friedrich Nietzsche's *Thus Spake Zarathustra*. There, too, you will find in immortal prose his obit on God, one of the more extraordinary gestures of self-importance in modern lit.

THE GOSPEL ACCORDING TO JEAN-PAUL SARTRE

Twentieth-century French philosopher Jean-Paul Sartre, a leading figure in the philosophic movement called existentialism, heeded the pronouncement of the nineteenth-century German philosopher Friedrich Nietzsche. "God is dead," Nietzsche had proclaimed.

No God, Thanks

Like Nietzsche, Sartre was an avowed atheist. Since, according to Sartre, no God exists to give meaning to life, life taken as a whole is meaningless. As existentialists are fond of saying, life is absurd. It has no purpose or intrinsic value because God does not stand outside the creation to infuse value into it.

The individual aspirations and works of men and women have no ultimate meaning, either. Our destiny at birth is death. Period. Although there's always a very, very slim chance that our works might outlive us, from the perspective of eternity, our efforts and our products are as fleeting and ephemeral as Ozymandias's memorial to himself—so much landfill in the making. It is much ado about nothing. Annihilation is the ultimate end: Coming into and passing through this life is a meaningless twitch, a mere spasm of absurdity. Still, thanks for buying this book before you died.

Are you experiencing a visceral rush of revulsion or nausea yet? If you are, the clinical diagnosis is incontrovertible: You are experiencing the early stages of what is called existential angst, or dread. So you need to do yourself a

FRED, SLY, AND JOHN: TRUE-GRIT PHILODESPERADOS

Too bad Friedrich Nietzsche wasn't born in the Wild West, where women were women and men chewed, spat, and riddled offensive and smelly cowpokes with rounds of cheap ammo. When a cowpuncher's horse broke a leg in those days, even though the steed was his best friend, he had to face the facts and put the critter out of its misery. No liberal bleeding-heart lamentations or do-gooder attempts to save the poor varmint's life. A tough guy had to do what a tough guy had to do. Nietzsche liked to flatter himself with the idea that he was a tough guy. He thought it took colossal courage to admit that there is no God and to look down life's barrel without flinching.

favor. Go out and get a big dose of humor. Take an intermission, get on the internet, read the funnies, watch the *Comedy Hour*, take a tranquilizer, or, if you're an ironic sort, read the headlines, but find something funny to brighten your mood before returning for the rest of the story. Existentialism can be, sorry to say, a bummer.

Inventing Nature

Although meaningless from the standpoint of eternity, human existence is unique according to Sartre and other existentialists. Every other thing—living and nonliving—acts in accordance with a nature that determines how it will behave. But human beings have no such nature. We are free to choose what we will become.

For Sartre, human life involves making choices. One of life's curses is that choice is inescapable. If you want to evade responsibility for your condition or the condition of your neighbor or the world by not getting involved, by not making a choice about some issue like capital punishment, then you are choosing not to choose. Neutrality is your choice, and like any other choice, neutrality has its consequences.

> Here's another tough guy's views on the meaning of life:
> . . . that's been a philosophy that I've embraced my whole life, the right to fail on your own terms because the possibilities of succeeding are so remote—maybe yes, that's a bonus—but fail. It relates to almost every good character I've ever played. I mean, Rambo was willing to die for an ideal. Rocky, he knows he can't win. He says, "I can't win." But he just wants to go the distance. That's how I've always felt, my whole life.
> —Sylvester (Sly) Stallone, interview with Mr. Showbiz.com.

> Jean-Paul Sartre was a bit of a tough guy himself. In World War II, he joined the French Resistance and fought against the Nazis.

You Are What You Decide You Are

Choose you must. Your choices give rise to your projects, which are manifested in the world through your behavior and your works. These concrete manifestations of your efforts, in turn, express your values. In a sense they express *you*—who you are and what you stand for. Although Sartre considered existence in itself absurd, he saw individual people acting as value givers to their own lives and to the universe surrounding them, infusing it with meaning and value that it lacks in itself. We, not God, are the authors of

CLIFFS NOTES, STAT!

Jean-Paul Sartre's greatest philosophic work is *Being and Nothingness*. The book is virtually impenetrable for first-time readers of philosophy. For more on Sartre, read a book *about* him, rather than one *by* him. His novels and plays are also more pleasant reads than are his philosophic tracts.

"HELL IS OTHER PEOPLE."

Besides being a leading philosopher of the twentieth century, Jean-Paul Sartre was also a literary figure, publishing novels and plays. *No Exit* is one of his most famous dramatic works. The drama is set in a hotel room—Sartre's literary depiction of hell. Three characters who have recently died are forced to occupy the room together. The character Garcin endures one of Sartre's more hellacious punishments for past sins. He hears the voices of associates in the world of the living as they interpret his behavior during World War II. He had tried to create the impression that his actions were noble, but now he has no more control over what others think of him, and they are judging him for what he was—a coward. He is dead and powerless to change their verdict. His case on earth is closed, and now it is subject to the mercy of others' interpretations. As Sartre said, "Hell is other people." For proof, visit Manhattan.

the meaning of our own existence. As Elvis Costello says, "Every day, I write the book."

Cheer Up . . . but Don't Get Carried Away

As a matter of fact, the projects that express the values that give our individual lives an apparent meaning oftentimes outlive us, bestowing on us a kind of cheap immortality, if your concept of immortality is, say, a century or so. The bridges we construct, the monuments we build, the children we raise, the social causes we fight for and that change our laws and lives—these works often outlast our brief stay on the planet, even if often only by a few years.

Just as well. . . . Sartre's existentialist version of immortality is not exactly what you might hope for, anyway. In the long run, our works are as mortal as we are, and they, too, will suffer the fate of Ozymandias's monument. In the interim, our legacy is not in our control. After we die, our works are our objective remains, and they are left for others to interpret and to give value and meaning to as they see fit. Our legacy is at their mercy, and nothing prevents them from treating your memory shabbily. Nevertheless, even devaluation is value, so individual lives have meaning and can be meaningful even after death—although, as people say, nothing lasts forever.

THE GOSPEL ACCORDING TO JOHN

. . . John Dewey, that is. Dewey (1859–1952) was a twentieth-century American philosopher and one of the founders of pragmatism, a philosophic school which originated in the United States at the end of the nineteenth century. Dewey, born the year that Charles Darwin published *On the Origin of Species,* started his academic career as a biologist. Only later did he become a philosopher.

Cheerful Atheism

He, too, was an atheist, and his position was, in respects, similar to Sartre's. But his attitude was more optimistic. Dewey would agree that human life does not have meaning in the sense that it serves God's purposes. He would also agree that the world is the outcome of mechanical processes and that human life is destined to ultimate destruction. But he would not agree that life lacks value on that account. Values are as much part of the universe as other properties. An apple can be as desirable as it is red and round. We experience the colors and sizes of things, and we experience their value, too, in the same way. When we value something, our valuing it is a fact; it is part of our experience. But merely desiring something does not make it *desirable,* and merely valuing something does not make it *valuable.*

The Snow White Corollary

For example, on perceiving an apple's sweet fragrance, redness, and roundness, Snow White found herself desiring it, but a few days later, she woke up to discover that it hadn't been as desirable as she had thought. It was metaphorically rotten and factually undesirable. If she had devalued it, she would have made the right judgment of its worth. For some people, it's an apple. For others, it's a philosophy.

Science with Teeth

Human beings lack a large arsenal of survival instincts and weaponry—no horns, no venomous poisons, no fangs or the like for tackling the problems and perils of life. Mike Tyson's teeth were weapon enough to make Evander Holyfield's ear cartilage an unholy sight, but we doubt that Tyson would be gutsy or nuts enough to go for a chunk of a lion's ear; nature's notion of disqualification is a lot less forgiving than the Nevada Boxing Commission's. Despite our unimpressive physical endowments, human beings can compensate. In the way that the giraffe's long neck stretches up to those tasty delicacies atop tall trees, so human intelligence is itself an evolutionary development with its own survival value. Having intelligence does not guarantee its efficient or effective use, however. People do some really dumb things. Luckily, nature is harsh, and many of these jamokes get weeded out of the gene pool. For Dewey, the best way to keep genetics working on behalf of your progeny is to form the habit of practicing the most advanced method for applying intelligence. In other words, if you want to get ahead, you have to think harder. That method is science. In science, the experimental method determines the truth of beliefs and theories, and knowledge accretes as scientists build on the findings of their predecessors. In this way, we progress.

What a Good Idea Will Get You

Using our intelligence, we can make good assessments about the way the world is and about the values it has. The process is the same in both cases. Your perceiving the redness of an apple does not make it so. The apple might be a Granny Smith, yet you perceive it to be red because you are color-blind. If other people show surprise and insist that the apple is green, you have some good reason to question your judgment. You can then perform tests to determine who is right. Scientific apparatuses measure the frequency of light emitted from the surfaces of objects. If the object is red, it will reflect light from its surface at one frequency; if green, at another.

Likewise, whether human life has value can also be tested in experience. Ask yourself, "What are the possible consequences that issue from human life?" Humanity may bring about its own destruction through deforestation or the annihilation of other species or weird reproductive patterns. History already records that humankind has been responsible for a seemingly never-ending parade of bloody wars, follies of gargantuan proportion, crimes against humanity, and infamies that defy comprehension. All this evidence counts against the value of human life. But we also need to take account of the love, decency, charity, and concern people show each other; of the development of civilization, art, music, the NFL, and even philosophy. Weighing the evidence, you might decide that human life does have value, hence meaning. Yet you might also understand that not all the evidence is in yet.

> **PUBLIC PROBLEMS**
>
> For a readable introduction to John Dewey's political and social philosophy, see his *Public and Its Problems*. For a more technical account of Dewey's theory of values as a quality encountered in experience, scan his *Experience and Nature*.

DO-IT-YOURSELF PHILOSOPHY

Okay, we've staked out three leading answers to the question, "What is the meaning of life?" You should be able to answer the question yourself by now. Write your answer here: _____

_____

For those unable to finish that essay question before the bell, here's more:

WHAT ELSE YOU KNOW AND DON'T KNOW ABOUT THE MEANING OF LIFE

Your response to our big question—"What is the meaning of life?"—may depend to some extent on your epistemology and your metaphysics. You may not realize that you hold epistemological and metaphysical beliefs, but you probably do. For example, some epistemological questions that are related to our big question are

> **Stare at these definitions:** Your *epistemology* is your theory of knowledge. Your *metaphysics* is your theory of what is fundamentally real.

- How do we acquire knowledge?
- Is it possible to *know* whether life has meaning?
- Is it possible to *know* what meaning life has?

Even if you haven't given these matters much thought, you probably have assumptions about them. You might, for example, assume that you can know what the meaning of life is. This assumption might motivate you to search for an answer. But if you're skeptical about whether the human mind is capable of answering the big question, you might be inclined to ponder instead the more urgent questions of our time: Did O.J. do it? Who will win the playoffs this year? Why did Slick Willie get away with it?"

Some metaphysical assumptions can also influence thinking on our big question. For example, if you happen to believe that God exists, you might also believe that God endows human life with purpose and meaning (the traditional view). If you think God doesn't exist, you can't consistently hold that God is the author of life's meaning. If life has meaning, its meaning must derive from another source.

IS THERE METHOD IN THE MADNESS OR MADNESS IN THE METHOD?

So you can see that in philosophy everything gets complicated *fast*. If you're going to stay on track, what you need is a plan, a scheme, a *method*.

This counts, because the methodology one uses to tackle questions can also be a big factor in influencing one's answers. Philosophers have a long history of squabbling about the right methodology for conducting philosophic investigations. Below are three approaches.

THREE METHODS OF PHILOSOPHIC ANALYSIS

THE METHOD . . .	. . . AND HOW IT AIMS TO TAME THE MADNESS
Pure reason	Socrates and René Descartes are good examples of philosophers who relied on pure reason. **The Socratic method:** Socrates was a kind of scruffy character who might easily have been arrested for vagrancy or loitering in New York City. He used to hang out in the agora, the marketplace in ancient Athens, and accost unsuspecting men with seemingly innocent questions like "Excuse me, but what is justice?" Then—ancient Athenians apparently having more free time than midtown execs—a dialogue would ensue. This dialogue format, captured by Plato, is what came to be known as the dialectical or Socratic method.

THE METHOD . . .	. . . AND HOW IT AIMS TO TAME THE MADNESS
Pure reason (*cont.*)	How it works: Acting as interrogator, Socrates would ply his partner with question after question. In attempting to answer, the responder would typically be reduced to aporia, a state of confusion that know-it-all types might have preferred to spare themselves by avoiding Socrates altogether.
	Once reducing his dialectical partners to aporia, Socrates often continued his interrogation, forcing his responders to dig deeper, discovering truths that they had been unaware lay inside themselves. Socrates likened his role in this process to that of a midwife because his questions elicited the truth much as the midwife brings forth an infant from within its mother's womb as the fruit of her pain and labor.
	Socrates' views on philosophic method were driven by his epistemology. Because he believed that all human beings have all knowledge stored in their minds at birth but at a subconscious level, knowledge had to be brought out rather than crammed in. Through interrogation, the Socratic (or dialectical) method draws out knowledge already present within.
	For a good illustration of the Socratic method in action, see Socrates' interrogation of the slave boy in Plato's *Meno*.
	The Cartesian method: René Descartes, a seventeenth-century French philosopher, mistrusted the senses, so he relied on his reason alone as a source of knowledge. Like a master mechanic, he inspected the tired old philosophy of his day, a Model T relic spilling oil and belching smoke everywhere. The danged thing had become a road hazard, getting in the way of those sleek technological marvels designed for environmental correctness, the *autobahn* and the Grand Prix. Descartes' verdict? No tune-up or quick trip to Midas could salvage this rusting antiquity. Only a complete bumper-to-bumper overhaul could save it from an ignominious end in some urban junkyard.
	In his *Meditations*, Descartes describes how he went about his gigantic task of disassembly and reassembly. He writes that he sat down by the fire in his study. Using nothing but his reason, he proceeded to dismantle traditional

THE METHOD . . .	. . . AND HOW IT AIMS TO TAME THE MADNESS
Pure reason (*cont.*)	philosophy from rear end to motor mount, after which he systematically rebuilt the whole thing with such careful craftsmanship as to ensure trouble-free performance—or so he thought.
	Descartes' charts: For more, see Descartes' *Rules for the Direction of the Mind* and his *Discourse on Method.*
Scientism	During the seventeenth century, science emerged as a major and later dominant force in investigations of nature. Science became so successful that many philosophers came to believe that philosophy should emulate scientific method. Philosophers who hold this kind of view are called positivists. The writings of Auguste Comte, a nineteenth-century French philosopher, motivated a twentieth-century movement in this direction. Both John Dewey and Bertrand Russell were positivistic in orientation. In the 1930s, a school of philosophers called logical positivists emerged. They held that philosophic problems that could not be solved by science or logic were pseudoproblems.
	For a readable account of the logical positivists' position, see Alfred Jules Ayer's *Language, Truth, and Logic.*
Ordinary language	Ordinary language philosophy is one orientation within the analytic tradition.
	Analytic philosophers believe that philosophic problems can be solved or dissolved through a process of analysis by which complex issues are broken down into simple parts. These simple elements are thought to be simple in the sense that they can not be further analyzed. They are inherently clear.
	The ordinary language tradition began with the English philosopher G. E. Moore (1873–1958), who defended a reliance on common sense. Moore thought that many perennial problems of philosophy resulted from language confusions that would be cleared up if people would stick to ordinary language. His astute use of ordinary language to dissolve long-standing philosophic problems gained many followers. A notable adherent was John L. Austin (1911–1960), who held the view that it's no accident that words in everyday language have grown to mean exactly what they

THE METHOD . . .	. . . AND HOW IT AIMS TO TAME THE MADNESS
Ordinary language (*cont.*)	mean over time—and that the words we commonly use, whether they be specific or vague, have come to be that way because they serve a useful purpose.
	Moore's views also influenced Bertrand Russell, whose own search for simples led him in another direction, and Ludwig Wittgenstein (1889–1951), who believed that anything that can be said can be said clearly and precisely. Due to Wittgenstein's influence, a lot of philosophy practiced in England and the United States since the 1940s has consisted of attempts to dispel philosophic questions by disentangling language confusions. Talk, talk, talk . . .

CLARITY IS A PEANO SONATA

Mathematician Giuseppi Peano (1852–1932) specified five rules for defining the series of natural numbers. How's this for brevity and clarity?

1. Zero is a number.
2. The successor of any number is always a number.
3. No two numbers have the same successor.
4. Zero is not the successor to any number.
5. If the above postulates are true for zero, and if the above postulates are also true for any other number (let's call it *n*) and *n*'s successor, then the above postulates are true for all numbers.

For many philosophers (perhaps Bertrand Russell foremost among them), the perspicuity of mathematical language became an ideal for philosophy to emulate.

HOW LORENA BOBBITT MISUSED OCCAM'S RAZOR

William of Occam (1285–1349) is purported to have once said, *"Entia non sunt multiplicanda praeter necessitatem."* Literally translated, the Latin means "Entities are not to be multiplied beyond necessity." Liberally translated, it means, "Keep it simple, stupid." As a Franciscan monk, Occam's sharp objections to multiplying beyond necessity must have nicked the church fathers' convictions too deeply, because he was accused of heresy before the pope and had to spend much of his adult life on the lam. A modern-day follower of Occam, Lorena Bobbitt was determined that her husband not multiply beyond necessity either. Despite Lorena's views, shorter is not inherently better. Nevertheless, Occam's razor has become a widely accepted dictum of science, which has a long tradition of striving for simplicity in theoretical formulations. Given two theories that equally explain some phenomenon, scientists—and many philosophers, too—feel obliged to adopt the simpler version.

POP QUIZ

As mentioned above, philosophers' primary tool is reason, and their primary tool of reason is logic. If you take the graduate record examinations (GREs) to qualify for admission to a graduate program in philosophy, you will have to score very high on the logic parts of the test. So let's administer an aptitude test to see if you have a future in the growing and dynamic field of philosophy. *No cheating, though.* Cover the right side of the page below. That's where the answers are. Directions: Determine whether the following arguments are good (valid) or bad (invalid). See above for a very very very brief refresher course in logic.

TEST YOUR PHILOSOPHY APTITUDE	
ARGUMENT	ANSWER
If God exists, then creation is perfect. God does exist, so creation is perfect.	This argument is valid. Its premises and conclusion are as follows: ■ If God exists, then creation is perfect. ■ God exists. ■ So creation is perfect. This argument has the logical form known as modus ponens: If X, then Y; therefore, Z. The second premise affirms the first part (the antecedent) of the first premise, which has an "If . . . then . . ." form. On this basis, the conclusion ("Z"), which is the consequent or "then" part of the first premise, is validly deduced.
If God exists, then Creation is perfect. God doesn't exist, so creation is imperfect.	This argument is invalid. It commits the formal fallacy of denying the antecedent. The term *formal* is used to describe the fallacy because the argument is an instance of the invalid logical form known as denying the antecedent: If _____, then _____. It is not the case that _____. So, it is not the case that _____.

ARGUMENT	ANSWER
	The first premise merely tells us what the state of the creation is in the event that God exists. It doesn't assert anything about the state of the universe if God does not exist. The universe could be perfect whether or not God exists. Consider an analogous argument. If you prepare for the chess game, you win. But suppose you don't prepare for the chess game. It doesn't follow that you lose. Plainly you might win even if you don't prepare. Your opponent might forfeit, for example.
Jean-Paul, you think that the universe is meaningless because God doesn't exist. You must be a communist, atheist jerk to think that way.	Remember this fallacy (page 4)? This third argument is an example of the informal fallacy *argumentum ad hominem*—attacking the person making the argument, rather than the argument itself. In the case of the second argument above, reasons were given to show you that the argument is invalid. But in the case of this third example, the person committing the fallacy does not give a good reason for rejecting Jean-Paul's reasoning. Instead, the person resorts to calling him names.
I bumped my head on the door yesterday, and I won the lottery. Whack me on the head again, *please!*	This reasoning is also invalid. It is an example of the informal fallacy of false cause, believing that something was the cause of an event simply because it preceded it.
Increasing the level of difficulty . . . Liar's paradox—answer true or false: This sentence is false.	Can you solve the following paradox? Rumor has it that Epimenides and Eubulides are to blame for this brand of mind bender, which is a member of the "semantic paradox" family. Although the liar's paradox has been presented in various forms, the one

ARGUMENT	ANSWER
	used here is a common version. The statement is paradoxical because if it is true, then it is false, and if it is false, then it is true.
	Bertrand Russell offered a solution to the paradox. According to his theory of types, the paradox is the result of the sentence being about itself. It is a blend of two types of statements that need to be distinguished. If we say, "Warblers are yellow," we are making a perfectly coherent statement about warblers. But if we say, "Warblers is an eight-letter word," we are making a very odd statement. Warblers are birds, not words. We correct the problem by using italics: "*Warblers* is an eight-letter word." This revised version makes clear that the statement is about a word rather than a bird. It belongs to a higher logical type, according to Russell. Confusing logical types can end in paradox.

THE GRAND AND GLORIOUS HISTORY OF ISMS

OR WOULD YOU PREFER FERRIS BUELLER'S PHILOSOPHY OF THE INGLORIOUS ISM?

Isms, in my opinion, are not good. A person should not believe in an ism. He should believe in himself. John Lennon said it on his first solo album. "I don't believe in Beatles; I just believe in me." A good point there. After all, he was the Walrus.

—Ferris Bueller,
   in the movie *Ferris Bueller's Day Off*

EVEN UNABOMBERS HAVE AN ISM

According to the book -*Ologies & -Isms: A Thematic Dictionary*, Luddism is the "belief of bands of early nineteenth-century English workmen [Luddites] that attempted to prevent the use of laborsaving machinery by destroying it." Of course, the Unabomber took a slightly different approach, destroying laborsaving management instead.

Philosophy is full of isms, general doctrines or ideologies. In a philosophic variant of Newton's third law of motion, isms seem to attract equal and opposite isms. Politics is a great example of an ism blood sport. In their marriage and on TV commercials, Republican Mary Matalin and Democrat James Carville champion their respective conservatism and liberalism in a senseless and shameless exhibition of contrarianism. Whether for good or ill, isms dot the landscape of philosophy, and novices can't hope to evade the philosophic claymores (a type of hidden and lethal land mine used in Vietnam) unless they know the philosophic lingo. So here's your

THE GRAND AND GLORIOUS ISMS OF METAPHYSICS
Monism
Defenders of the ism:
Thomas Hobbes (1588–1679)
Bishop George Berkeley (1685–1753)

Monism is the metaphysical theory that the world is made up of only one kind of stuff or fundamental reality. (Believe it or not, *stuff* is an accepted technical term in metaphysics.)

So how come the world doesn't look like one stuff, you ask? The answer is simple. There is a difference between appearance and reality. The world *appears* to be made up of many types of things, but *in reality,* it isn't what it appears to be. If, for example, the universe is composed of subatomic particles, then the watermelons, rock stars, and Caribbean islands that populate the world as it appears to us may be mere appearances of an underlying reality—the subatomic particles of which they are made. As Janis Joplin said, "It's all the same damn thing, man."

Materialism
Materialism is one type of monism. Thomas Hobbes, one of its chief defenders, was a down-to-earth sort who just couldn't get into the spirit. Or maybe it was the other way around: the spirit couldn't get into him. Anyway, although he was not entirely consistent, he was credited with advancing the view that the one and only reality is matter. Everything mattered to him except nothing, which is nothing, because it doesn't matter.

Idealism

Idealism is another kind of monism. Idealists believe that the one fundamental reality is made up of minds or spirits and their ideas, a theory widely believed in Eastern cultures. **Caution:** Philosophical idealism is not to be confused with the sort of idealism that one associates with having high-minded ideals or values. In fact, for our purposes, philosophic idealism might be thought of as "idea-ism," or the theory that only ideas and the minds or spirits that have them are real. According to the Bishop George Berkeley, *esse est percipi* ("to be is to be perceived"). So what happens when a tree falls in the forest but no one is around to hear it? Answer: Nothing, unless God perceives it. Berkeley's cryptic reply to Hobbes's materialism: "No matter."

Dualism
Defender of the ism:
René Descartes (1596–1650)

Dualism is the metaphysical theory that there are two and only two types of fundamental reality. Descartes defends a familiar version. He holds that the two fundamental metaphysical orders are mind (spirit) and matter. Human beings are composites of the two, which are (conveniently for us) temporarily hooked together in this life but disconnected on death, the one to fertilize the flora and the other to take up residency in whatever realm of spiritual existence disembodied minds occupy. According to the Gospel, you have a choice of rent-controlled living quarters: heaven (located uptown, a peaceful and happy community where free lyre concerts are held nightly) or hell (located in a sleazy downtown section, a riotous fun-loving den of rock concerts, lust, and iniquity, as well as horrendous pain and despair brought on by the virulent strains of the social diseases that run rampant there).

Pluralism
Defender of the ism:
Aristotle (384–322 B.C.E.)

Pluralism is the metaphysical theory that the world is made up of a plurality of types of fundamental reality. A plurality means three or more, up to infinity.

Aristotle believed that our planet is composed of four fundamental types of reality: air, earth, fire, and water. For Aristotle, the four earthly elements were subject to constant change or corruption, by which he did not mean that the four elements had a future in politics or that they would never pass an IRS audit. What he meant is that everything is subject to alteration in one of four ways: change of quantity (losing or gaining weight, for example), quality (dyeing your hair blond), place (moving to Chicago), and substance (dying and becoming plain old earth). In each case, a thing or one of its states alters, ceasing to be as it was before.

THE GRAND AND GLORIOUS ISMS OF EPISTEMOLOGY
A Note of Rare Humility

Both rationalism and empiricism have long traditions. As the theories developed over the centuries, so did the versions of them. A brief generalization about these theories will not do justice to the subtleties of their many versions. What follows is a crude summation. (Luckily, in the *Pocket Professor,* a crude summation is bound to go unnoticed.) So take what follows to be a very preliminary account intended to give you an idea of central themes.

Not Every Idea Is a Great Concept—or Even a Good Idea

To us civilians, most concepts are not revolutionary or dramatic. Each one of them may be nothing more than a plain old idea. However, inside this book, you can use the words *concept* and *idea* interchangeably, so don't get thrown when we talk about concepts and how we come by them. When you think of your poor suffering dog, Growl, who is this moment getting shots at the veterinarian, Growl is not before you, but your concept of her is. Your concept is a surrogate in your mind by which you think of Growl even when she's not around (at least according to a traditional view). Note that Growl and your idea of her are very different. Growl growls; your idea doesn't. But . . .

A Cautionary Note

Although appropriate for now, the above clarification may be misleading if you go on to read the works of historical figures in philosophy on your own. In the history of philosophy, the terms *idea* and *concept* are not used uniformly. For the sake of simplicity and brevity, such refinements are ignored here. But if you go on to further reading, look out for differences in usage. Don't assume that the same term in the mouth of one philosopher has the same meaning when another philosopher mouths it. These clowns don't get their stories straight.

Where Do Ideas Hang Out?

If you are asked where your idea of Growl is located, odds are you're going to say "in my head." But is the idea in your head in the way that your brain is in your head? Imagine you need brain surgery, and a neurosurgeon saws into your cranium to expose your otherwise shy and reclusive brain for all to see. Using her five senses, she will be able to observe your brain: she'll see, feel, hear, smell, or—excuse us for the gruesome reminder of Marie Prevost—taste your brain. If she systematically pokes around your gray matter, looking here and looking there, do you suppose she'll observe your idea of Growl hanging out among the folds? According to a traditional view, she can't. Your concept of Growl is part of your mental life; it is not the sort of thing that can be part or property of a material thing like a brain. Your idea's proper place of residence is a mind, a mental entity. You are the only person who can observe the contents of your mind, and you can do so only through an internal and private act of mental awareness. Other philosophers have challenged this traditional view. They believe that ideas are physical in the sense that they are states or properties of brains and nervous systems. When the good doctor peers at your brain, she can observe your idea because it is nothing more than the brain or nervous system in a certain state. Whatever ideas are and wherever they reside, how do we manage to get them *in* us? To answer this question is to offer a theory of how ideas or concepts get formed. Such a theory is a theory of concept formation. In the history of philosophy, two main theories have been advanced. Two main isms have tried to explain.

A BODY OF THOUGHT

As indicated above in the discussion of dualism, René Descartes distinguished mind and body so radically as to make them mutually exclusive. In this regard, he is a seminal thinker who shaped Western thinking about minds and bodies. See his *Meditations*. For a physicalist account that challenges the Cartesian tradition, check out John Jamieson Carswell Smart's *Philosophy and Scientific Realism*.

Rationalism
Defenders of the ism:
Plato, René Descartes, and Immanuel Kant

A paranoid lot, rationalists are by and large mistrustful of experience, most particularly sense experience, which, they think, misleads us. Straight sticks dipped in water appear bent; the sun, if you rely strictly on what you see, appears to be a foot to a foot and a half in diameter, and water that appears to lie tantalizingly a half mile ahead on a sun-baked Mojave Desert interstate turns out to be a mere mirage. If the formation of our concepts depended on experience, then we would have good reason to be dubious about the reliability of our ideas. A house is, after all, no more trustworthy than its foundation.

Plato was a pure rationalist. He believed that all our concepts are implanted in our minds before birth. To understand his theory of concept formation, let's start with our old friend Growl, a very big dog. Peep, a little chihuahua, is also a dog but tiny in comparison to Growl. Together they are a kind of doggy-world Mutt-and-Jeff duo (whose relationship is, for obvious reasons, strictly Platonic).

When Growl and Peep play together, you are able to recognize and distinguish the two of them even though you also recognize both of them to be dogs. Presumably, to accomplish this feat, you apply your concept *dog* much as you would use a picture on a post office wall to identify one of the 10 most wanted outlaws. You compare suspects to the photograph, and if one of them resembles the photograph closely enough, you call the FBI to claim your reward.

But your concept *dog* can't work exactly the way the photograph does. A pictured dog, whether a picture of Growl or Peep or any other particular dog, will display a particular figure. It will depict a large or small dog, or one some size in between. If you use a photograph to recognize both Growl and Peep as dogs, then it will fail. If the pictured dog is large, then Peep won't be a dog; if small, Growl won't be a dog, and if in between, either one or both won't be a dog. So how do you manage to use your concept *dog* to recognize both Growl and Peep as dogs? Plato offered a rationalistic answer.

Before you were born, according to Plato's theory, your disembodied soul inhabited a changeless world, parallel in respects to our own but existing outside time and space. There, without the benefit of any senses, using, so to speak, its mind's eye, your soul apprehended some very odd entities, which Plato called forms. These forms are neither physical nor mental things. Rather, they belong to another order of reality altogether. One of these forms is dogness, which exhibits the essence of being a dog. This essence does not include any particular properties like being three feet tall or weighing 80 pounds or having black hair, since a canine might lack any of these properties yet still be a dog. Rather, the form dogness exhibits all and only those properties that are essential to anything's being a dog.

In a blink of its mind's eye, your soul snapped, as it were, a mental picture of dogness and imprinted it in its internal album. But eager for experience, your soul did not stop there. It apprehended every form, developing and storing a concept of each. In this way, you acquired your concepts of *dog, house, doghouse, Martian, casaba, baseball player, tooth, cloud, unicorn, mugwump* (Are you one?), and every other concept that could ever come into your mind. After experiencing all these wonders, your soul, perhaps bored with changelessness and yearning for new adventures, transmigrated from the world of forms to this world, carrying within it all the concepts it had acquired in its former existence. Having secured control-tower clearance to land, it glided to its runway, which turned out to be your mother's birth canal, whereupon you were born a slimy, howling infant. But instead of being a know-it-all because all your concepts filled your conscious mind at birth, you, for some peculiar reason Plato does not explain—perhaps the trauma of birth, forget everything you experienced previously in the world of forms, which explains why babies who are really bursting with information appear to be such dim-witted know-nothings who need to learn everything from scratch.

Luckily, your forgotten concepts do not vanish altogether. Rather, they take up residence in the recesses of your memory. There they sit like minor-league baseball players collecting splinters on dugout benches waiting for their call up to the bigs. Then when the right circumstances occur, one of your concepts gets the nod. Jogged out of memory (sometimes due to a sensory experience), it makes its rookie appearance in conscious awareness, adding to the home-team lineup the power needed to make sense of experience.

According to Plato, sensory experience is not *the* or even *a* source of your concepts, though, coincidentally, it sometimes aids us by prompting concepts to emerge out of memory. According to his theory of concept formation, all the concepts your mind will ever acquire are already present in it before you have a single experience in this world. Concepts are, for Plato, *a priori,* literally acquired prior to experience. (But for our purposes, you're better off to think of *a priori* concepts as ones that are formed independently of experience in this world.)

René Descartes, another rationalist, did not believe that Plato's world of forms existed. He thought God zapped our concepts into us, so God, not experience, is the real originator of our ideas.

Empiricism
Defenders of the ism:
Aristotle, John Locke, and David Hume

Empiricists are a more trusting lot. They think experience is *the*— or at least *a*—source of our ideas. Aristotle (384–322 B.C.E.) attacked the rationalism of his esteemed but dead and defenseless mentor Plato. How's *that* for gratitude? Aristotle contended that our ideas get formed as a result of sense experience. Objects impress the senses much like a king's signet ring makes an actual physical impression. After being dipped in hot wax and pressed onto parchment, the ring leaves its impression there. Once formed, a sensory impression can inform the mind by impressing its form (in Aristotle's lingo, the "sensible form" or "sensible species") onto the intellect. Once transplanted to the mind, the sensible form becomes an intelligible form or concept. And that's how you acquire your ideas, according to Aristotle.

John Locke (1632–1704), the founder of a philosophic school called Traditional British Empiricism, is credited with reviving empiricism as the philosophic counterpart to the scientific movement of his day. He believed that the mind is at birth a tabula rasa or blank slate. Imagine a piece of blank paper in a typewriter. (No. Scratch that. If you're a reader under sixteen, you probably have no clue, i.e. no concept, of what a typewriter is. Why? Because, as any robust red-blooded empiricist would hasten to tell you, you've probably never experienced one of those museum pieces.) So imagine a blank screen on your monitor. It remains blank, a tabula rasa, until you start pressing keys on the keyboard. Keyboarding is, so to speak, an electronic form of creating impressions. What keyboarding is to the blank monitor, experience is to your _____. (Fill in the blank.) You're right! Why? Because you're experienced in how analogies work.

Locke advanced an empiricist account of how concepts get formed in us. His fellow British empiricist David Hume (1711–1776) improved and clarified Locke's theory with a slick, boffo version. For Hume, experience begins with impressions. Slothful readers will be happy to learn that they can get many impressions without having to work for them. Sometimes—like wax or a blank slate—people just get impressed. Unless you are among the reading dead, you are this very instant experiencing some degree of warmth in your hands. You didn't ask for or seek this impression. But there it is all the same, forming part of your experience. Sometimes impressions are sensory. Your visual, sound, tactile, olfactory, gustatory, and kinesthetic impressions comprise this group. But you also experience your own mental functions as they occur. In this way you acquire impressions of willing, hoping, judging, perceiving, and the like. Pretty impressive so far, don't you think?

Impressions, Hume tells us, are forceful, lively, and vivacious, one and all. If we happened to be sadistic authors, we might stick a pin into your unsuspecting fleshy forefinger. You would then receive an impression—*ouch!* That pain you are experiencing is vivid or, as Hume says, forceful, lively, and vivacious.

Now suppose a day has passed. You feel better. But you find yourself remembering the unhappy incident and the pain you had experienced the day before. Your recollected pain is no longer forceful, lively, or vivacious. According to Hume, you have formed an idea of it. A concept, according to Hume, is nothing but a remembered impression. That is why, being a good Humean, you no doubt prefer your idea of a pain to the pain itself, if given a choice.

According to Hume, all impressions are simple little experiential atoms of color, taste, sound, touch, smell, and mental activity. When you recollect a simple impression, you form the corresponding simple idea. You receive an impression of red, for example, recall it, and, presto! You form the simple idea *red*. In like fashion, you form your ideas of green, spherricity, sweetness, firmness, and so on. If you put simple ideas like these together in the right ways, you form complex ideas, like your idea of *apple,* a nifty little feat of mental gymnastics.

Hume believed that your mind can perform three main functions: It can combine, analyze, and transpose. By *combining* simple ideas, it forms complex ones like *apple,* which you can then baptize *apple.* Your friend Gunter, forming the same complex idea in his mind, might call it *apfel* instead. Once you have combined simple ideas to form complex ones, your mind can *analyze* these complexes, breaking them down again into the simple ideas from which they were composed in the first place. Your mind can also *transpose* ideas. For example, it can take your simple idea *pink,* which happens to be a constituent of your complex idea of *Porky Pig,* and it can substitute it for your simple idea *gray,* which is a simple part of your complex idea *elephant.* Through this remarkable mental ability, you are able to form your idea of a pink elephant (and to concoct other equally fabulous fictions). The *Pocket Professor's* law of transposition: The level of consumption of hallucinogens and alcohol is an inverse relation to sobriety and a direct relation to the propensity to transpose ideas. In brief, this is Hume's empiricistic theory of how we get ideas, both simple and complex.

What tools do we have at our disposal to acquire knowledge?

Reason Leads the Way

Rationalists Plato and René Descartes put their trust in pure reason as *the* tool for acquiring knowledge. Their mistrust of the senses inclined them in this direction. Reason, they believed, is a remarkable tool, able to apprehend the truth of propositions directly and immediately without the senses acting as intermediaries. In rationalistic circles, the mind's capacity to perform such mentalistic feats goes by various names: intuition (a favorite), insight, and seeing (mentally, that is), among others.

If you happen to be one of those stubborn, anal-retentive types who can swallow rationalism about as fast as you can chug-a-lug castor oil, here's a proposition that ought to induce you to open wide: "Either James Earl Ray murdered Martin Luther King Jr. or he didn't." To know that this proposition is true, would you have to be an eyewitness to the deed? No indeed! Just use your noodle, think a moment about the proposition, and you will *see* that it is true and couldn't be otherwise.

Traditionally rationalists did not have to make careful distinctions between types of knowledge. Since they were married to pure reason and in this regard were monogamous, whatever pure reason apprehended to be true was true, or so they thought. If you had the good sense (obviously, in the sense of being wise) to believe only what pure reason revealed to you to be true, you would acquire only knowledge and never be mistaken.

The Senses Have Something to Add

Empiricists do not dispute the importance of reason in acquiring certain types of knowledge, but they think that it is not the only tool at our disposal. They think the senses are a source of knowledge, too. If I parade Growl and Peep before you and ask you what the dogs' colors are, you will answer correctly: "Growl is black and Peep is brown." But how did you come by such knowledge? Simple answer: you observed their colors with your visual sense. In Hume's terminology, you received impressions of the dogs' colors, and you acquired some empirical knowledge in consequence.

But imagine that you had been blind since birth. Then you would never have seen Growl and Peep with your own two eyes. You would have only smelled and petted them. Do you suppose that any amount of pure thought, no matter how energetically concentrated on Growl and Peep, would reveal their colors to you? To acquire such information, you rely on more than pure reason. You use your senses.

According to David Hume's version of empiricism, human beings have four instead of only one tool for acquiring knowledge: pure reason, as the rationalists contended, plus observation, memory, and experimental inference or induction, as it came to be called. Observation occurs when you receive impressions, as you do when, for example, you smell and pet Growl and Peep. You acquire knowledge using memory when you remember prior impressions, and you get knowledge by induction when you generalize on the basis of having similar experiences. If you travel worldwide observing crows, a million in total, all of which turn out to be black, you are entitled to use induction to infer that *all* crows are black. Induction is an empiricist's tool for inferring generalizations based on experience.

Confess! You're an empiricist. You think you use your senses to acquire knowledge of the world. Right? Then read on. There's more. We again select David Hume's version to represent the empiricist cause. The Wily Scot believed there were two and only two types of knowledge: analytic and synthetic. (Actually, Hume's terminology was longer and more cumbersome, so we adopt Immanuel Kant's more concise language.)

Analytic knowledge is knowledge that Hume would say is known by pure reason or by sheer mental analysis alone. The statement "All bachelors are unmarried" is true. The concept *unmarried* is part of the concept *bachelor*. The assertion "All unmarried males are unmarried" is necessarily true but not exactly earthshaking news. You don't need experience to establish its truth, and no amount of experience could ever falsify it, either.

Hume conceded this much to the rationalists. Analytic truths are known *a priori*. Unaided by sensory experience, pure reason gives us knowledge of such truths. But—here's the bad news—analytic truths are trivial, according to Hume. They tell us nothing significant about the world. They are true merely as a result of the part–whole relationship between concepts making up the assertion. If pure reason were our only tool for acquiring knowledge, the sum of human wisdom would be an aggregation of trivialities. (Math-anxious readers will be pleased to know that Hume tended to regard mathematical knowledge as analytic, hence also trivial.)

But, according to Hume, there is a second type of knowledge—synthetic knowledge. Take the statement "All bachelors are bald." No amount of sheer reasoning will ever reveal the truth or falsity of the claim. If you want proof of this, you must venture out, like Diogenes, searching for just one hairy bachelor, perhaps a recent graduate of the Rogaine restorative regimen, a bachelor with at least one healthy, functioning follicle on his otherwise expansive pate. If you find just one such embodiment of male vanity, then you will presumably be quick-witted enough to know that not all bachelors are bald. Through their sensory experience, they will have acquired one piece of significant (although, again, not earthshaking), information about the world.

The rationalists are just wrong. At least some knowledge does derive from sensory experience.

In the way that Hume, a spokesperson for empiricism, had to make concessions to rationalism, Immanuel Kant (1724–1804) made concessions to empiricism, so much so that some philosophers consider him essentially an empiricist and others consider him a hybrid—an empiricorationalist. Kant agreed with Hume about analytic and synthetic knowledge, but he claims that there is a third type that Hume did not recognize—synthetic *a priori* knowledge. What's that, you ask.

One example is a principle Kant lifted from Euclidean geometry: "A straight line is the shortest distance between two points." Kant insisted that this proposition is not analytic. We don't know it in the same way we come to know that all bachelors are unmarried. *Shortness* is not part of the concept *straightness*. Straight lines can, after all, be long as well as short. You can analyze the concept *straightness* from today to doomsday, but you'll never find the concept *shortness* contained in it, so this truth of geometry is not known by an act of pure mental analysis alone.

Yet, Kant believed, it is a truth of mathematics. So, if you happen to be a dyed-in-the-wool empiricist and you believe that there are only two types of knowledge—analytic and synthetic—you might be inclined to infer that this geometric truth is an example of synthetic knowledge. Experience certainly teaches us that the shortest distance between two points is a straight line. Every time you encounter two points, a straight line drawn between them is always shorter than any other alternative. Having had such uniform experience and lots of it, you are entitled to make use of induction, David Hume's rule of empirical generalization, to infer with great confidence that a straight line is *always* the shortest distance between two points. Experience is your teacher and guide.

So empiricism seems vindicated. Euclid's principle turns out not to be odd at all; it's just an example of good old empiricist synthetic knowledge. Kant has served up a phony example of synthetic *a priori* knowledge, not a genuine all-beef Whopper but an ersatz imposter—you know, one of those tofu look-alikes—or so it would seem.

But gentle Herr Professor Kant, leading his quiet and virtuous life at the University of Königsberg, would have been indignant at the accusation that he had not produced the real McCoy. If he were alive, he would have admonished us for drawing conclusions too hastily. A Kantian parlor trick: If you're going to draw anything, draw two random points on a piece of paper. Now draw a straight line between those two points. Next try to draw another line shorter still but not straight. You will see (but with what—your eyes or your mind?), almost instantly, not just that you didn't but that you *couldn't*. It is impossible for a shorter line than the straight one to be drawn. The claim that the shortest is the straightest is, Kant tells us, a necessary truth. Experience can justify belief in truths about the way the world is but not about the way it must be. So experience cannot be the source of such knowledge, yet we know it.

Hume made the mistake of thinking there are only two types of knowledge when there are really three: analytic, synthetic, and synthetic *a priori* (as the previous example shows). He also made the mistake of thinking that the mind has only four tools for acquiring knowledge: pure reason using mental analysis to attain analytic knowledge, on the one hand, and observation, memory, and induction to gain synthetic knowledge, on the other. Kant claims a fifth tool of mind—transcendental deduction—another form of mental apprehension by which the mind (unaided by experience) sees that synthetic *a priori* judgments are true. Rationalism is vindicated, at least to an extent.

Seen from this vantage point, Hume might come off as not only a wily but a thrifty Scot, an-idea-saved-is-an-idea-earned type of philosophic tightwad who wielded Occam's razor with reckless disregard for rationalism's life and limb. But the saga does not end here.

THE GRAND AND GLORIOUS ISMS OF ETHICS
Absolutism
Defenders of the ism:
Judaism, Catholicism, Protestantism, Plato, Aristotle
Ethical absolutism is the theory that there are moral principles, standards, or commandments by virtue of which actions are right or wrong or people are good or bad irrespective of any other qualifying or extenuating conditions or circumstances. What it is, man.

Judeo-Christian heritage: In the West, the collective influence of Judaism and classical Greek philosophy yielded a powerful although partly unintentional alliance of faith and philosophy that resulted in a long and distinguished tradition in support of absolutistic doctrine. Taken at face value, the biblical injunction "Thou shalt not kill" is straightforward and unequivocal. If the Ten Commandments were taken literally, just as stated, they would be absolute moral imperatives in consequence of which many more of us would land on the kindling pile of eternal hellfire than we might like to believe. Killing would be wrong, for example, whether in self-defense or time of war. There would be no mitigating or special circumstances under which killing would be right or permissible. The moral law determines what is right and wrong and who is good or bad. Come Judgment Day, malefactors can drag their high-priced shysters to represent them at the pearly gates, but no amount of subtle thought, whining, special pleading, or recounting of special circumstances (my-mother-didn't-love-me kind of blather) will do the sinner a smidgen of good. All the protesting and persiflage will be so much sputtering in the face of the intractable, irreversible, and immutable force of the moral absolute. Wrong is wrong and bad is bad. Either the petitioners obeyed the rules and thought and acted as they were supposed to, or they didn't. *Finito.* End of story! Next!

Relativism
Defenders of the ism
Protagoras, Friedrich Nietzsche

Ethical or moral relativism denies that absolute ethical norms, commandments, or standards exist. *Ethical subjectivism,* an extreme brand of ethical relativism, is the theory that moral worth depends on the beliefs, feelings, or attitudes of individual people. Since such states of mind can alter over time, the moral worth of a given action or person is not fixed once for all. No act is right or wrong and no human life absolutely good or bad. An act that a person thinks right and is therefore right today might be thought wrong and hence be wrong tomorrow.

Cultural relativism is the theory that whether actions are right or wrong depends on cultural mores, which differ from culture to culture and are merely social inventions intrinsic to the societies that invent them. The theory has found its most ardent defenders not among philosophers but among anthropologists.

> **Man at work:** Check out the groundbreaking work of Melville Jean Herskovits (1895–1963) in his *Man and His Works: Cultural Anthropology.*

As twentieth-century anthropologists studied different cultures, they discovered a remarkable diversity of customs and mores among them. They also found that they would often misunderstand a culture's mores or practices if they applied the theories, concepts, and values of their own cultures to the societies they were studying. Since mores are thought to be intrinsic to whatever culture invents them, using an outside culture's moral standards as a basis for evaluating their moral worth is to apply an inappropriate standard. (Using the term *wrong* here would be wrong. Get it?)

Let's suppose there is a society of Thormafridites, who worship Thor, the god of thunder, and who ritually sacrifice a cherubic virgin the third Thursday (or *Thors*day) of every month. As long as the sacrifices took place faithfully, as the faithful insisted they must, experience had shown that Thor's wrath, in the form of violent thunderstorms, was intermittent and rare. On the basis of this evidence, killing the virgins was, for the Thormafridites, an ethical obligation and sacred duty. According to cultural relativism, killing virgins is right in Thormafriditic society, although wrong in, say, Christian culture.

The two cultures' ethical beliefs are incompatible, so surely one must be correct and the other mistaken. Not so, according to cultural relativists. The two cultures' beliefs are merely different; neither is mistaken. For a Thormafridite, killing virgins is right under certain circumstances; in Christian circles it is always wrong. But any attempt to adjudicate between them by applying, for example, Christian principles, is simply inappropriate . . . or worse, an example of what is these days referred to as cultural imperialism.

Protagoras

Protagoras (481?–411 B.C.E.) was an ethical subjectivist. He also was a leader of the Sophist school of philosophers, who despite having no school building to call their own were the Western world's first paid teachers. They traveled the Hellespont seeking and accepting gratuities from all comers willing to pay the tidy sum of 14 drachmas to be taught whatever it is they wanted to know.

Made to measure: Protagoras is best known for proclaiming that "Man is the measure of all things . . ." People form beliefs. As we all know, their beliefs can be in opposition. Saddam Hussein believes that Iraq is being persecuted; President Bill Clinton disagrees. Who's right? Protagoras, if he were here, would seem to believe that both are! People experience the world differently. They form their beliefs on the basis of their divergent perceptions and perspectives. No objective basis exists for determining whether one perspective is more veridical than another. If, for example, Yasir Arafat were to judge that Saddam's perspective is more legitimate than Clinton's, Yasir would be relying on his perspective. He's right, too. Of course he might come to change his mind, in which case his previously held belief would have been true at the time that he believed it, but it is false now that he has reconsidered. In effect, to say that a proposition is true is to make an incomplete assertion. One should say that the proposition is true for a person X at time T. This way of asserting that a statement is true makes explicit that its truth is relative to a given subject and her beliefs at a specific time. In this sense, Protagoras' subjectivism is a form of relativism, but a radical form.

Plato and Aristotle

Plato was aghast at what he took to be Protagoras' epistemological perversity, not merely because Protagoras' theory was false but because it encouraged people and whole societies and states to aspire to having no better guide to their conduct than their own beliefs, no matter how ill founded. The notion that the truth has no measure other than oneself makes a mockery of the human quest to know what is good, right, just, true, and beautiful—in short, to know what makes life worth living.

WHAT PLATO KNEW Plato believed that knowledge—including ethical knowledge—has a basis outside ourselves. Goodness itself exists independently, abiding eternally in the world of forms. People are good or bad insofar as they do or do not exemplify the form of the good, which is an absolute standard. Again, there are no ifs, ands, or buts about it. Either you exemplify the form or you don't.

According to Plato, the good is the highest of the forms, and knowledge of it is the highest knowledge to which human beings can aspire. In principle, we earthlings can tell the difference

> Like Protagoras, Gorgias was a Sophist. Read Plato's dialogue *Gorgias* for a bird's-eye view of how insidious sophism can be. Then check out Gorgias' views in the discussion of justice in the *Republic*.

between good and bad because each of us bears within us our idea of the good acquired when our souls resided in the world of forms. Our concept acts as a surrogate against which we can measure and compare ourselves to determine whether we are good or bad. Our status is a matter of fact. The verdict depends on whether we exemplify the form of the good. For some odd reason that Plato does not explain, our concept of the good is also the most difficult for us to recall, so anyone's claim to have such knowledge is *prima facie* suspect. Yet if some saintly sage (Buddha, Mother Teresa, Joe Schlavinsky, the deli owner on 33rd Street, or L. Ron Hubbard) happened to have his concept of the good poof into his consciousness, then he or she would, Plato assures us, know the good and, what's more, do it. As Plato said, to know the good is to do the good. In effect, all wickedness is, he thought, ignorance. Adolf Hitler, Jack the Ripper, Idi Amin, and Pol Pot were misinformed.

OLD-FASHIONED VIRTUES   Plato and Aristotle use the term *virtue* in an unfashionable way. Before the sexual revolution, *virtue* was used to refer to the intact presence of a woman's chastity. Plato's and Aristotle's use of the term belongs to an even more bygone era. For them, virtue is an excellence. If Peep the pup, for example, happens to be an excellent instance of his breed, his owner might show him in the Chihuahua International Dog Show, to be held next April 26, in Mexico City. Peep has a good chance to take first prize because as a matter of fact, he excels at being a chihuahua. He has the excellences or virtues appropriate to being the best of breed, including, say, being small, quick, even tempered, and obedient. Today we might say that Peep is a model chihuahua, kind of a Platonic ideal.

SOUL? MAN   Like Peep, Peep's owner belongs to a species with a nature—in her case, human nature. The word for *soul* in Greek is *anima,* what animates the body, making it alive and prompting it to do whatever it does characteristically. Peep and Growl have canine souls; their masters, human souls. Following Plato, Aristotle thought that a thing's soul defines its nature. When Growl and Peep bark at mail deliverers, chase cats, and hover around the dinner table awaiting stray morsels, they are doing what comes naturally for creatures animated by a doggy soul.

THE THREE-PART SOUL   Plato theorized that the human being has a tripartite soul:

- Appetite
- Emotion
- Reason

Appetite gives rise to our desire for food, sex, and offspring. Emotion stokes our passions, such as courage, jealousy, love, and hatred. Reason makes us curious, leading to deliberation and, well, reasoning. When we act in accordance with our appetites, emotions, and reason, we perform functions that are natural to a human being. These natural functions sometimes conflict, however. Our appetites and passions, for example, sometimes overpower our reason to our own detriment. Using reason, people can understand, for example, that they are consuming unreasonable amounts of food, smoking when they shouldn't, and remaining in dead-end relationships with loser creeps whom they should have booted out long ago and who will bring them only grief in the long run. Yet for all reason's wise counsel, some people—slaves to appetite or passion—seem powerless to stop. The stomach and heart are in control as if they had the head firmly by the nose and could drag it about wherever and whenever they wanted.

BALANCING ACT   According to Plato, a person needs a well-balanced and ordered soul. In the proper ordering of the soul's three parts, reason would be in control but allow the other two parts and the corresponding natural functions their due in the proper measure. As Plato said basically, all things in moderation. Reason needs to act as the moderator permitting us to do what comes naturally but in the right amount—the (oftentimes elusive) midpoint between excess and deficiency, between too much and too little—the golden mean, as it is called.

According to Aristotle, virtue is the habit of choosing the midpoint. Some people seem incapable of preventing self-indulgence or stinginess of sentiment. Others—the virtuous ones—seem to hit the bull's-eye with remarkable regularity. If you happen to be one of those benighted and disharmonious souls who can't help reaching for more than you need, then you should acquire the habit of moderation. But note that acquiring it is one thing; passing it on to others who need it is another. According to Aristotle, virtue can be learned but not taught. "Run that by me one more time," you demand incredulously. "Learned but not taught? Did you say 'learned but not taught?'"

ROLL A MODEL Aristotle theorized that one acquires the habit of virtue as a result of being in the company of good people who habitually choose in moderation. Yet modeling works in some people and not in others. So how people come to learn virtue from others is a mystery. This much is clear, though: People do not acquire the habit of virtue from anyone's teaching it to them. Learning the habit of choosing in moderation is a matter of character development.

> **Mean feat:** In Aristotle's ethics, Plato's golden mean becomes the absolute standard against which virtue, right, and wrong can be measured.

PLATO'S PROOF OF THE THEORY OF FORMS FROM DEGREES OF PERFECTION

Here's how Plato met the challenge using some fast talk and a couple of sticks, without once disguising himself as Protagoras:

1. Let *a* and *b* be two different sticks that appear equal in length. *(Given)*
   (a) _____
   (b) _____
2. We know that *a* and *b* fall short of being perfectly equal—that is, perfect equality. *(Premise)*
3. So we know what perfect equality is. *(2)*
4. We would not know what perfect equality is if perfect equality did not exist. *(Premise)*
5. So perfect equality exists. *(4, 3)*
6. Perfect equality does not exist in the world of particulars. *(Premise)*
7. Therefore, perfect equality exists outside the world of particulars. *(6)*

Your character is expressed in your behavior, which is recognizable because you behave in characteristic ways. Alas, the habit of virtue is not a lesson to be learned or a habit easily acquired. So, all you parents and someday-to-be parents out there, listen up! Aristotle, a forerunner of Dr. Haim Ginott and Dr. Benjamin Spock rolled into one, had he lived long enough, might have put his point in more modern lingo: It isn't what you say; it's what you do.

Friedrich Nietzsche

Friedrich Nietzsche (1844–1900) rejected classical regard for reason. He also rejected the classical Greek and the Judeo-Christian views that there is an absolute standard by which to judge whether actions are right or wrong and persons are good or bad.

FLEX-ETHICS   Nietzsche's doctoral studies had been in classical philology, the study of literature and how words are used in literature, before he turned to philosophy as his principal occupation. His philologic investigations led him to read extensively about ancient cultures, many of which predated Christianity. He learned that different societies believe different theories about the origin of the world and nature, and they likewise offer different prescriptions for human conduct. For Nietzsche, each society's ethical codes are merely expressions of its values and are not inferior to the Judeo-Christian injunctions. Their purpose is the same: to conform behavior to society's values. Ethical codes, he wrote, are merely instruments for exacting obedience of some preferred sort. As such, they are not absolute criteria for determining moral worth. Instead of reason controlling appetite and emotion to create a well-ordered soul, reason is the slave of the passions (a sentiment David Hume expressed eloquently a century earlier).

MEN OF UNREASON   In this regard, philosophers have not behaved like paragons of reason, according to Nietzsche, who claimed—no doubt because he wasn't Christian himself—that for the most part philosophers have acted as Christian apologists. Nietzsche dubbed them lawyers because they have no interest in the truth (that is, in whether their client committed the crime). All they care about is winning the case. To this end, they develop arcane and elaborate intellectual schemes to gain assent to whatever it is they personally value and desire.

For Nietzsche, there were no moral absolutes. If you've ever wondered why human beings and different societies have such varying ethical beliefs, Nietzsche's answer is plain. Individuals and societies have different moralities because they have different interests to defend—just as Nietzsche had his.

Consequentialism Nonconsequentialism and Egoism
Defenders of the First Ism:
Jeremy Bentham (1784–1832) and
John Stuart Mill (1806–1873)
Defender of the Second Ism:
Immanuel Kant (1724–1804)

Consequentialism is the ethical theory that actions are right or wrong depending on their consequences. A very influential form of consequentialism is utilitarianism, which is discussed below, after a brief digression.

Nonconsequentialism is the ethical theory that acts are right or wrong and persons moral or immoral independently of any consequences. Put negatively, consequences are not factors in determining the ethical value of actions or people.

Egoism is a related theory, which takes two forms. Ethical egoism is the theory that people *ought to* act in their own interest. This theory is sometimes confused with psychological egoism, which is the theory that people *do in fact* act in their own interest. Friedrich Nietzsche was both a psychological and an ethical egoist.

Jeremy Bentham

Jeremy Bentham is credited with being the father of utilitarianism, an ethical and political theory very influential in eighteenth- and nineteenth-century England. Although versions of utilitarianism vary widely, in general utilitarians subscribe to some form of

> **THREE MORALS**
>
> - The consequences of an action may be more far reaching than its perpetrator is aware. *Ask President Bill Clinton.*
>
> - An action may fail short of its purpose. *Ask the House Republicans.*
>
> - A person's purpose can be achieved or foiled by accident. *Ask Linda Tripp.*
>
> Scottish Romantic poet Robert Burns put the point this way. "The best-laid schemes o' mice an' men gang aft agley" (ofttimes go astray). Keep these morals in mind as you read about the consequentialists and the nonconsequentialists below.

the principle of utility: The right act is the one which contributes to the greatest good of the greatest number.

WHAT'S YOUR PLEASURE?   Under the influence of British empiricism (Hume, chiefly), Bentham wanted to establish an ethics grounded in experience and verifiable in the manner in which scientific beliefs are empirically verified. He opens his *Introduction to the Principles of Morals and Legislation* with this famous remark: "Nature has placed mankind under the governance of two masters, *pain and pleasure*. It is to them alone to point out what we ought to do, as well as to determine what we shall do."

Bentham considered the highest good to be happiness, by which he meant pleasure, and the greatest evil to be unhappiness, by which he meant pain. His equation of happiness with pleasure makes him a hedonist. Like egoism, hedonism has a psychological and an ethical form. Bentham believed that pleasure is the intrinsic good (psychological version) that is and ought to be (ethical version) what we seek.

WHAT NOW? DO THE MATH!

Bentham thought that pain and pleasure could be measured and assigned unit values he called lots. He thought he could contrive a utilitarian calculus, a kind of, as he said, moral thermometer or moral arithmetic. Morality could then become a science. He identified seven factors to be taken into account when evaluating how many lots to assign a given act:

- Intensity—the degree of pleasure or pain an action produces
- Duration—how long the pleasure or pain lasts
- Certainty—how assured one is that a consequence of an act will be a pain or a pleasure
- Propinquity—the proximity or nearness of the source of pleasure or pain
- Fecundity—how many consequences to which an action is likely to give rise
- Purity—whether an act gives rise to only pleasurable or only painful (that is, unmixed) consequences
- Extent—the number of people affected by a particular action

In this way, using simple arithmetic, Bentham thought he could calculate with accuracy which courses of action would be the right ones to follow for an individual or for humanity as a whole.

PRIVATE MORALITY'S NOT A BIG DEAL COMPARED TO PUBLIC MORALITY
When only the agent, the person performing an act, is affected, then the greatest happiness that determines the right course of action is the greatest happiness of the sole individual involved. However, if the consequences affect other persons immediately—or, owing to the fecundity of the act, remotely—then the greatest happiness of the greatest number determines the right course of action.

DOING THE PLEASURE MATH   What mattered for Bentham, then (with some exceptions), were the consequences of an action and the extent to which they conduce the greatest happiness (pleasure) of the greatest number. Intentions are inconsequential. What counts is what is empirically countable—the quantity of pleasure or pain produced. Qualitative considerations are irrelevant. You don't get any bonus points for creating beauty or any other traditionally esteemed quality. In other words, if watching *Married With Children* gives you more pleasure than watching *Masterpiece Theatre,* watching Al Bundy is the right thing to do.

For reasons that should be pretty obvious by now, Bentham's utilitarianism caused so much profound and sustained mental anguish among theorists that it is questionable whether he was right on utilitarian grounds to have put forth his theory in the first place. Who was he giving pleasure to with this high-falutin' theory?

John Stuart Mill

John Stuart Mill's father, James Mill, was an influential philosopher of his day and an associate and ally of Jeremy Bentham, who was a frequent visitor to the Mill household. The elder Mill subjected his son at a very early age to a rigorous and demanding educational experiment in home schooling, emphasizing the classics, languages, history, and scientific and logical analysis. Like many experiments, this one resulted in good news and bad news. The good news: Young John became the brilliant thinker his father had hoped for. The bad news: He ended up a basket case.

At age 20, he found himself either on the verge (or over the edge) of a nervous breakdown. Seeking comfort, he turned to the Romantic poets of the eighteenth century and his own day, most notably William Wordsworth, Samuel Taylor Coleridge, and Thomas Carlyle. These literary figures were eloquent and implacable foes of the

---

RUNNING BENTHAM THROUGH MILL

As John Stuart Mill said with remarkable economy of thought, "It is better to be a human being dissatisfied than a pig satisfied." According to Bentham's moral arithmetic, a human life mixed with pain doesn't measure up to the life of a pig wallowing contentedly in a lifetime supply of slop. Yet, as Mill pointed out (perhaps naïvely), few people would choose to be Miss Piggy even if they were assured that their lives as swine would be uninterrupted pleasure. This putative fact shows that people take more than quantity of pleasure and pain into account when they assess worth. If it is true that we seek happiness above all things, what makes us happy is, for Mill, not just more pleasure but also the kind and quality of the pleasure. The pleasures of the intellect, the emotions, and the imagination are what Mill called higher pleasures. These pleasures outweigh the pleasures of sensation. Correct assessment of moral worth needs to take into account quality as well as quantity. According to Mill, more is not necessarily better. To salvage Bentham's moral calculus, Mill needed a reliable method for assigning quantitative values to qualitative pleasures. But he gave no empirical basis for making such assignments, opting instead for that old rationalist standby—intuition. There's a lesson in all this: beware of your defenders. And maybe you *should* watch *Masterpiece Theatre* instead of *Married With Children*.

---

scientism and technology sweeping Europe. They feared science would overthrow sentiment (the inspiration of their muse) in favor of what they might have characterized as bloodless and unfeeling rationality. In the Romantics' view, science was rational analysis run amok. Too much head . . . too little heart.

Mill's emotional crisis did not cause him to abandon Bentham's utilitarianism, which he had adopted at an earlier age. Instead he sought to correct what he deemed its excesses. Following Bentham, he held that happiness is to be understood in terms of pleasure, unhappiness in terms of pain. The right act is the one that brings about the greatest happiness of the greatest number. Bentham had thought that right and wrong could be calculated using pure quantitative analysis alone, a scheme Mill debunked.

Immanuel Kant, the Original Good Will Hunting

Consequences can never tell us what is right, according to Immanuel Kant. Sometimes events unfold in the way we want them to, sometimes not. Good intentions can have bad consequences, and bad intentions can also have good consequences. In the Bill

Clinton–Monica Lewinsky affair, for example, Monica's intentions might have been good. A bad consequence was the impeachment of the president. The president's intentions might have been bad, but a good consequence was an approval rating that defied gravity. It's unlikely that the president sought that good consequence by plotting with bad intention.

Recognizing that outcomes are not in our control, Kant repudiated consequentialism. What matters for him is that one's heart be pure. That we comply with the moral law is required, but compliance is not enough. Ya gotta believe! Why we comply counts, too. According to Kant, the only thing that is good without qualification is a good will. For Kant, a good will is one that has as its purpose or intention to act purely out of respect for the moral law, to do what reason reveals to be right regardless of the consequences, including the consequences for oneself. A good will functions as if it were a disinterested or impartial party, acting irrespective of ulterior motives and without regard for outcomes. So even if an act has as a consequence the greatest happiness of the greatest number in history, if the intentions informing the act are wicked, the act is not good. For Kant, intentions determine moral worth.

The Christian religion has divergent tendencies regarding goodness. One tendency emphasizes having a good heart, acting out of pure motivations without regard for reward or punishment as consequences of one's behavior. Another tendency warns of divine punishment if one is disobedient, encouraging people to think prudentially. In your heart, you may desire to perpetrate all manner of wicked deeds, yet you might restrain yourself because you fear divine punishment. In the case of the latter, it doesn't take a brain surgeon to figure that one night in the sack with the latest Hollywood heartthrob isn't worth being torched to a billion

> **You bet your (eternal) life:** Check out Blaise Pascal's *Pensées* on this point. According to Pascal's wager, a betting person would believe in God because it's a better wager than being atheistic or agnostic, considering among the other relevant factors the punishment to be endured if you choose not to believe and you're wrong.

> **Tell-all:** Saint Augustine argued in favor of a field-of-dreams approach to faith for hearts that lack it. Act like a Christian, he counseled, and the heart will follow. For more on St. Augustine's personal struggle to find faith, read his *Confessions*.

degrees Fahrenheit forever. Love is fleeting; hell is forever. These tendencies are not incompatible, however. Submission out of fear does not necessarily condemn those who are reluctantly obedient.

FEAR NOT! Kant rejects the view that God would exact obedience out of fear, for such a god would be unworthy of respect, more a dictator than a divinity. After a hard night's debauchery, Nero, for example, awakens in a foul mood and on that account decrees that 100 Christian parents shall on this day sacrifice their firstborn to the lions. His minions are dispatched and succeed in rounding up 100 Christians who, out of fear, render unto Caesar what is Caesar's. But Nero's might does not make his law right or his authority worthy of respect. God would be no better than Nero if He, She, or It commanded obedience from fear. God's laws should be respected not because God has the power to punish us but because God's laws are respectworthy.

According to Kant, the Lord is no tyrant. God's perfect intellect knows what is right, and for this reason alone It wills Itself to act in accordance with the law. Part of God's perfection is the perfect attunement of Its will to Its moral reason. What God's reason knows to be right, God wills.

THE CATEGORICAL IMPERATIVE Kant called the moral law that reason commands us to respect and obey the categorical imperative. His use of the term *categorical* is rich with meaning, some of which will become clearer after you have read about Kant in the Philoso-

---

WHAT KANT'S MORAL LAW MEANS TO YOU: BEHAVE YOURSELF!

Kant believed that the moral law is binding on every person. Good intentions are ones formed out of respect for the moral law. This moral law is, according to Kant, a commandment incumbent on every person to obey. Every person has reason, and reason determines how we ought to behave as rational beings. So we know what we are obliged to do, and we all feel our obligations as a sense of duty. If we were perfectly rational, we would behave as reason dictates. But we are not God and we are not perfectly rational. We are also flesh and blood and subject to the temptations of the body. Unlike God, whose will is exquisitely attuned to Its reason, we experience desires that prompt us to disregard our duty and to do what our desires dictate instead. In such instances, we act unreasonably and immorally (and may wake up with a moral and/or physical hangover).

phy Hall of Fame (pages 111–112). Here we will explain only part of its connotation.

When politicians are accused of taking bribes, odds are they will emphatically deny the charges using language something like this: "I categorically deny these false and politically motivated accusations against me." By categorically denying the allegations, the politician repudiates the claim absolutely; she contends that there is no truth whatever to the accusations; the charges are utterly and completely unfounded; they are without qualification false—no ifs, ands, or buts about it. Applied to Kant's moral law, the term *categorical* means that the law imposes on everyone moral obligations that are binding, regardless of circumstances or conditions.

The moral law is as unconditional as unconditional surrender. A losing general forced to surrender unconditionally is not in a position to bargain. "What if we wait two hours?" "What if you allow us to keep our small arms?" "What if . . ." These what ifs are attempts to impose conditions and to avert unconditional surrender. If the surrender is in fact unconditional, there are no ifs. Likewise, a categorical imperative is a commandment that obligates unconditionally and without any qualifications. In other words, there are no "get out of jail free" cards. You must follow the rules, or suffer the consequences.

TWO WAYS TO DO YOUR DUTY

By now you are no doubt, categorically and without qualification, bursting to know what Kant's categorical imperative or moral law is and how our reason uses it to figure out what our duties are. It turns out that Kant gave several versions of his categorical imperative (by some counts five). We'll examine two, both of which Kant expressed with biblical solemnity.

CATEGORICAL IMPERATIVE: VERSION 1 (PARAPHRASED)

Act only in accordance with those maxims which you could at the same time will without contradiction to become a universal law of nature.

A maxim is a general rule or principle of conduct: Do a good deed every day; Think no evil thoughts; Turn the other cheek; Render unto Caesar what is Caesar's," and the like. Version 1 of Kant's categorical imperative is a rule that allows us to judge which maxims or rules of conduct we should follow.

Consider an example. You have been waiting on a long line to buy a ticket to a movie. After 30 minutes on line, you are 10 people away from the ticket booth. A big, nasty-looking guy—Rocco, we'll call him—walks up, cuts into the front of the line, and buys his ticket without having to wait a nanosecond. Presumably Rocco has a maxim like the following to guide his selfish conduct:

> Whenever there is a line, I break in so that I don't have to be inconvenienced by waiting.

Let's see how Kant might apply his categorical imperative to Rocco's maxim. Note that the maxim as stated applies only to Rocky himself and to no one else. It is a subjective or personal rule. According to version 1 of Kant's categorical imperative, we need to reformulate Rocco's personal maxim as a universal law of nature, kind of like the law of gravity. [As the story goes, Isaac Newton once sat beneath an apple tree awaiting enlightenment until it arrived in the unexpected form of an apple coming loose, falling on his head, and knocking some sense into him. Smart guy that he was, he saw more than an isolated individual experience regarding his head and the particular apple. So he formed a general law of nature describing a universal force acting on all bodies.] The process of generalizing that Kant recommends is called "universalizing." To universalize Rocco's maxim so that it has the character of a universal law of nature, we reformulate it as follows:

> Every one should cut into line whenever doing otherwise would inconvenience them.

If this revised maxim were a universal law as inexorable as the law of gravity, then everyone behind Rocco would instantly, automatically, persistently, and en masse try to cut in front of him, pushing him back in the line. Instead of gaining the advantage he wants for himself, he ends up in an endless pushing and shoving match with everyone fighting to be first. According to Kant, Rocco's maxim—when universalized—contradicts itself in the sense that it becomes self-defeating. It confounds Rocco's motivation for breaking into line in the first place. People like Rocco who act on maxims that contradict themselves when universalized are being bad, and their actions are wrong . . . and what's more they know it, the jerks!

Standard, from the factory: Although you might never have heard of the categorical imperative before, it is, according to Kant, part of your mental makeup, and it operates within you whether you recognize or understand it. When Rocco cuts in front of you, you may not deliberately and consciously go through the process of universalizing his maxim to see whether it is self-defeating, but this bit of mental gymnastics is going on in your mind, nevertheless. You just know that this kind of selfish behavior is wrong and that it violates ethical principles regarding respect for others. Every person's mind works this same way, according to the Kant, so that not only you but every witness to the event, including Rocco himself, knows that the act was wrong. But he happens to be one of those persons whose selfish desires override his reason. His intentions are self-serving; he is bad and his action is wrong.

Version 2 of the categorical imperative will have a more familiar ring than version 1.

CATEGORICAL IMPERATIVE: VERSION 2 (PARAPHRASED)

So act as to treat humanity, whether in another person or yourself, in every case as an end, never as a means only.

Treat others as ends, not means, Kant admonished us. In short, don't use people. When Rocco cut in line, he was not showing respect for others. To show respect is to treat others (including yourself) as you would like to be treated. Kant's categorical imperative turns out to be remarkably like the Golden Rule: Do unto others as you would have others do unto you. Masters may abuse their slaves and find all sorts of reasons to make their behavior seem moral, but they cannot escape the truth that resides within themselves. Using others for your own ends is categorically wrong.

If people act out of respect for the moral law, treating others and themselves with respect, then they are good; otherwise, not. Intentions are what count. A well-intended person can bring about unintended consequences, and an ill-intentioned person can inadvertently bring about happy consequences, so according to Kant, consequences are inconsequential. What matters is whether the person intended to do the right thing.

Enough of those guys. Read on, below, for another Big Philosophical Question.

WHAT IS THE LIFE WORTH LIVING?

This really big question, which Plato raised nearly 2,500 years ago, motivated much of his philosophic career. What's at stake in the question? Imagine borrowing to the limit of your gold credit card to get into a really hot stock deal you heard about from a friend of a friend—you know, the double-your-money-quick, once-in-a-lifetime kind of deal. To you, the stakes might seem about as high as they get, considering everything you are about to risk. But have we got a flash for you: Your really big gamble is small potatoes in comparison to what's at stake in Plato's big question, which carries the wallop of a Muhammad Ali left hook to the spiritual solar plexus. So snap on your protective headgear, tuck in your chin, and prepare to take some punishment.

Ask yourself, "Am I leading a life worth living?" Have the guts and decency to insist on philosophic discipline, honesty, and courage. Not allowed are any wishy-washy guessing ("I think so") or any Clintonian weaseling ("I remain agnostic on the issue."). If you don't know for sure that you are leading a life worth living, then for all you know, you aren't!

What if, on reflection, you reach the disturbing conclusion that your life so far has been a flop and not worth the living. Then what? Well, your thoughts might proceed as if by some perverse yet natural sequence of feverish rumination to another really big question, perhaps the biggest one of them all, "Why keep on going?" or, as William Shakespeare's Hamlet famously put it, "To be or not to be, that is the question."

By now you should be able to see that the stakes involved in this big question are higher than the stakes in your ill-advised stock gamble. If you worry that your life is not worth living, you have to make some life choices, among them to move to a state where suicide is legal, to get your head shrunk at the rate of $150.00 per 50-minute hour, or, as Plato recommended, to examine your life and then to change it from its present unworthy and sorry state to one worth living. Given this particular set of choices (not the only ones available, by the way), you might think to yourself, "What the hell, let's give Plato a try." Although the outcome is as uncertain as psychotherapy, it's cheaper and (unlike suicide) it's not final. Your other options still remain open. So what do you have to lose? And if you should be successful in discovering the life worth living, wouldn't you then straightaway pursue it, turning away from morbid thoughts to the positive task of living?

Now that the stakes are clear and you are all cranked up, suited up, helmeted, and ready to punch the lights out of the big question, we suggest that you cross your arms, form a big *T*, and take a strategic time-out. As explained earlier, the best way to hit a question is not always to bang your noggin straight into it. Plato warned that the unexamined life is not worth living. The *Pocket Professor* offers this credo as a variation:

The unexamined question is not worth answering.

Plato's really big question has some noteworthy features:

- **It's a specific question.** You might think that Plato would launch his inquiry with the question "Is there a life worth living?" Instead, he asks a different question: "What is the life worth living?" His use of the definite description presupposes that there is such a life. It's a given.
- **Plato's use of the definite description also implies that there is one and only one life worth living.** Lots of people today would gladly settle for any life worth living, on the assumption that there can be more than one, perhaps many, such lives. Like Shirley MacLaine, there's more where that came from.
- **Plato's question contains an ambiguity, although his meaning is clear enough.** When Plato asks what is the life worth living, he is not referring to one and only one particular life but rather to one and only one type of life. Remember Sir Gawain of King Arthur's knights of the Round Table? Arthur sends the pure (some say dull-witted) Gawain on a medieval Mission Impossible to find the Holy Grail. The Grail was the chalice from which Christ drank at his last supper. Regrettably, Gawain had not troubled himself with clarifying his mission (a violation of the *Pocket Professor*'s credo) before undertaking it. Contemporary philosophers draw a distinction between tokens and types. A grail is a type of chalice; each individual chalice—the Holy Grail, for example—is a token, a specific and unique instance of the type. To succeed, Gawain cannot bring back any token of the type, any chalice whatever. Not even a very good counterfeit will do. He has to find the one and only chalice that graced Christ's lips at that fateful Passover seder. No other chalice, no other token of the type, will do. Although Gawain is pure of heart and fearless, his task is more than daunting. He must find the proverbial (in this case, sacred) needle in the haystack. Misunderstanding his mission, however, he returned with a cheap imitation of the grail picked up in a Constantinople back-alley tourist trap specializing in Christian artifacts. As you can imagine, Arthur was not pleased and sent the hapless Gawain back out to find the genuine article. Gawain was not so

dumb that he didn't know the limitations of his own intelligence. He knew he couldn't tell a fake from the real thing, so like the son who multiplied his talents, he returned with a wagonload of chalices, none of which turned out to be the Holy Grail. After two decades of going and coming in this way, receiving rebuke and chastisement, and sallying forth again, Gawain grew old and despondent. A merciful Arthur, recognizing at last the futility and folly of the quest, relieved the good knight of his duty, which out of sheer indifference and inadvertence fell to the Green Knight, whom some thought a sorcerer and others, even worse, a philosopher.

Like Arthur's charge to Gawain, Plato's question is ambiguous. Once clarified, it turns out to be less daunting, although no pushover. When correctly understood, his question becomes "What is the one and only one type of life worth living?" In fact, had Plato searched and searched high and low, in houses and haystacks, and then finally discovered the one and only one token of the life worth living, he'd have been mightily disappointed. Suppose this remarkable life had turned out to be Homer's. Then it would already have been lived centuries earlier, and no one else, including Plato, would ever be able to lead it. But what Plato sought was not *the life* worth living but *the type of life* worth living. Since any token of this type would be such a life, any number of people could lead it, including you. At least you could try.

- **Note that the kind of life for which Plato was searching needed to be only worth living; it didn't have to be perfect.** As Longfellow observed with poetic eloquence and imprecision: "Into each life some rain must fall." With due deference to the poet, lives do not necessarily include pains and disappointments, although as a matter of fact virtually all lives do. Yet lives can be worth living anyhow. What matters is whether over the long haul the qualities that count in favor of making a life worth living outweigh in an appropriate sense the features that count against it.

- **Polls don't matter.** The great majority of people are apparently convinced that their lives are worth living. Despite the most deplorable and wretched conditions under which so many live, the vast majority of human beings cling to life with remarkable tenacity. Yet, for Plato, thinking your life worth living doesn't make it so. Either your life has whatever it is that makes it worth living or it doesn't.

On the basis of the above analysis, we can change Plato's question to make it clearer—although not necessarily more palatable to the modern mind:

> *What is the one and only one type of life that is on balance and over the long haul worth living?*

SIX ALL-TIME FAVORITE CANDIDATES FOR THE *TYPE* OF LIFE WORTH LIVING

People have advanced a profusion of diverse and extravagant answers regarding the type of life worth living. Our picks for the really big six are examined below with all the irreverence their shallowness deserves.

Proposition 1: *Wealth* Is What Makes Life Worth Living

This popular answer to the big question frequently prompts such snappy, sappy, knee-jerk clichés as "Money can't buy you love" and "Money can't buy you health." Such replies may satisfy an egalitarian's wish for justice in a world that distributes wealth unevenly, but are they true? Ask yourself, "How is it possible that a computer geek like Bill Gates, who doesn't have a Brad Pitt face and who can't chuck a football one tenth as far as Joe Montana, can become as rich as Midas, find and marry the love of his life, and, if she gets a little sniffle, buy the Centers for Disease Control and Prevention just to be sure that a runny nose doesn't become a torrent and metastasize into something really serious, like the 24-hour flu? Cute and catchy rejoinders to proposition 1 are facile, and they have a lot of explaining to do.

Is wealth sufficient? To go about evaluating claims like this, philosophers often make use of the technical distinction between necessary conditions and sufficient conditions. For example, a necessary condition for a life worth living is breathing: you need to breathe in order to be leading any kind of life at all. But breathing does not suffice for a life worth living. If it did, every respiring human life-form walking the face of the Earth would be leading such a life, including the likes of Adolf Hitler, Tori Spelling, Pol Pot, Bart Simpson, and the Manson twins, Marilyn and Charles. It's a noxious thought, offensive to the cultivated moral sense—which may explain why its odiousness has eluded millions.

THE TROJAN EXAMPLE

As evidence that wealth is not sufficient for a life worth living, consider the story of Helen of Troy, who was reputed to be the most beautiful woman in the world, circa 1184 B.C.E. A Trojan prince named Paris stole Helen from her husband, King Menelaus. Although not as rich as Midas (or Bill Gates), Menelaus was doing all right, and if wealth *were* sufficient, he should have been able to live a life worth living with or without Helen. But wealth did *not* suffice. Crazed with love, Menelaus launched a thousand ships in an effort to get her back, by all accounts a pretty spectacular and world-class display of affection and evidence that wealth bereft of love does not make a life worth living.

Of course, Menelaus has his detractors, whose spin on the whole episode is very different. Some claim that he didn't give a fig for Helen and was glad to be rid of her. She was vain and profligate. One of Menelaus' closest and most trusted confidants revealed that his royal highness had on more than one occasion exclaimed peevishly that Helen was as good an example as one could find of a life not worth living. Secretly, he was ecstatic that that fool Paris now had the millstone around his neck. So the war that launched a thousand ships was not about Helen. (Menelaus' wealth had in fact already procured him the love of a couple hundred women whom he admired and adored for both their brains and their beauty.) It was about honor or, if you wish to be uncharitable, it was about the Greek version of machismo—in particular, the male aversion to being cuckolded.

Regardless of which side of history you are on, the result is the same. Menelaus' wealth was not enough to provide him with a life worth living. It was not a sufficient condition. He also needed either love or honor.

> The source: Check out Homer's *Iliad* for as good an account as one is likely to get on the true reasons for the Trojan War. There are dozens of translations, but Richmond Lattimore's is particularly pleasing.

Proposition 2: *Health* Is What Makes Life Worth Living

Most people would agree that health is a good thing and worth pursuing, yet it is neither a necessary condition nor a sufficient condition. You don't have to be healthy in order to lead a life worth living. For example, Stephen Hawking, the renowned physicist who suffers from advanced Lou Gehrig's disease (amyotrophic lateral sclerosis), is by most accounts leading a life worth living despite his ill health. Health alone, however, is not a sufficient condition. There are lots of healthy people serving life without parole.

Proposition 3: *Immortality* Is What Makes Life Worth Living

Hey, it's a concept. After all, like Doctor Faustus, lots of people would eagerly give their souls to the devil for the chance to live forever. But if one's life is not worth living in the first place, living it longer, even eternally, in the same way, is not going to improve it. Although longevity does give sinners more time to become saints, it also gives saints more time to become sinners. What matters most is not the duration but the character of the life you lead during the time allotted to you. As a philosopher might say, immorality is neither a necessary condition nor a sufficient condition of a life worth living. Besides, living forever would get, er, old. Even religious constructs of an eternal life don't propose that it be *this* one.

Proposition 4: *Beauty and Attractiveness* Make Life Worth Living

If this is your position, I'd advise you to get over it. Remember, everyone gets the face they deserve at age 40. To paraphrase Fran Lebowitz, if you're lucky enough to be good looking as a teenager, take a lot of pictures. Says Socrates, "Beauty is a short-lived reign."

Proposition 5: *Honor and Fame* Are What Make Life Worth Living

This candidate for a life worth living needs clarification before it can be irreverently rejected. Honor and fame are not identical. People like Attila the Hun and Charles Manson have fame because they are infamous. Fame is not a sufficient condition for a life worth living. The basis for the fame matters.

So honor is the more likely candidate. But honor consists of the esteem of others, which can be given or withheld. Honorable people can be denied honors due them, and dishonorable people can receive undeserved honors like former president Richard Nixon or Benedict Arnold before their misdeeds and character became public knowledge.

Perhaps what the defenders of proposition 5 have in mind is that an honorable life is worth living regardless of whether others bestow honors (deserved or undeserved) on it. If so, two issues arise: What is being honorable? Is being honorable a necessary and sufficient condition for a life worth living?

Proposition 6: *Pleasure* Is What Makes a Life Worth Living

Pleasure comes in many specific forms. Some hedonists think that pleasure in any form whatever makes a life worth living. (See Jeremy Bentham and John Stuart Mill's reply, pages 55–58.) Others may have specific pleasures in mind, such as the following:

- **The life worth living involves going for the gusto**, which consists of guzzling yourself into a blind stupor punctuated with occasional but forceful blows to the old melon using as a blunt instrument an unopened can of Bud, and then feeling the cool, sudsy spray slide down your stubbled cheeks to soak into your Acme Tools muscle shirt, there to take up residence forever. Then to perfect the moment, from the depths of your bloated belly, you liberate a mass of vile and loathsome vapors that erupt with such remarkable force as to shatter the silence of the night, drowning out the celestial harmonies of the entire Mormon Tabernacle Choir in concert at the church two doors down from your den. Now *that's* a life worth living. Hey, it don't get better'n that.

- **The life worth living is lived in boxers.** Normal-size men and women have to wonder about the rarefied air up there above the rim where Michael Jordan worked his basketball magic, experiencing the rush of a 40-inch vertical leap in defiance of gravity as well as uninterrupted victory. After a .200 batting average for a Chicago White Sox farm club taught him that a professional baseball career did not offer enough pleasure to make life worth living, he embarked on a personal quest for a model hedonist, someone whom he might emulate in his pursuit of lifelong pleasure, even after his retirement from his athletic career. Apparently he found such a mahatma (great soul) living in Hollywood. In an earnest effort to guide kids the world over in the direction of ultimate pleasure and the life worth living, Jordan had this to say about his newly found guru: "I like the way Bugs [Bunny] leads his life, and if I could go through life like him, that'd be great."

▪ **Pleasure happens.** As evidence that philosophers are not necessarily more wise or less inane than athletes, Bertrand Russell offered this rebuff to the life of the mind: "I do not believe that science per se is an adequate source of happiness, nor do I think my own scientific outlook has contributed very greatly to my own happiness, which I attribute to defecating twice a day with unfailing regularity." In itself, the regularity of Russell's bowels might not be sufficient for a life worth living, but it's hard to imagine a life worth living without such.

▪ **In contemporary industrialized society, the mother of all candidates for the specific pleasure that makes a life worth living: sex and sexuality?** This revolutionary turnabout in attitudes toward matters once thought taboo is the handiwork of two extraordinarily influential figures—Sigmund Freud and Levi Strauss. Freud made people aware of the libidinous forces motivating their behavior, a theory that westernized men and women have been zealously endeavoring to prove true ever since. Levi Strauss, the onetime manufacturer of rugged and serviceable farm apparel, invented jeans and with them, *buns*—male buns, female buns, voluptuous buns, firm and athletic buns, wiggly and jiggly buns, but most importantly, very tightly wrapped buns. Universally, buns are now considered so much a necessary condition of sex and sexuality and consequently the life worth living that a youngish woman with a thinnish and relatively attractive body who wiggles her way into a pair of jeans after consuming a particular brand of breakfast cereal can examine herself very closely, from this angle and that, in front of a full-length mirror while uttering such narcissistic profundities as "hum" and "huh," and TV watchers the world over understand and recognize her as one hot (as she says, in a later version, "dangerous") lady who has at her beck and call a life worth living, for which reason her viewers have consumed tons of her favorite cereal in the hope that it will do for them what it has done for her.

We could go on in this way caricaturing the many pleasures people seek in their unexamined attempts to lead a life worth living.

The books worth reading: For a detailed discussion of answers regarding the type of life worth living, see Aristotle's *Politics* and his *Nicomachean Ethics*.

But in the immortal words of one of Bugs Bunny's best buddies whose wisdom has always consisted in knowing when enough is enough, "Uh-tha-uh-tha-uh-that's all, folks!"—at least so far as pleasure is concerned.

PLATO'S ANSWER

So are you pumped, psyched, ready for wisdom to be revealed in a flash of psychedelic classical brilliance? Get ready. Here it comes, an ultimate truth pared down to the bare basics. What type of life is worth living? Plato's answer: *a happy life.*

Okay, so it's obvious.

But living about 400 years before Christ, Plato had no concept of the Christian afterlife that took over a millennium after Christ's death. The traditional Greek view of heaven and hell was much less dazzling and dreadful. Hades, the last resting place of the dead, was a rather dull and dreary hangout in comparison to the Christian hereafter of cherubim and angel choirs on the one hand and a fiery torture chamber on the other. Although Plato was himself uncertain as to whether an afterlife really awaited him, he nourished the hope that he would one day abide in Hades and pass time there with some of the great heroes and thinkers of the past. However, absent a Christian's notion of heavenly bliss, his chief interest was secular—happiness and the life worth living during his there-and-then existence on earth. This emphasis on the secular ought to strike a sympathetic chord among the many denizens of contemporary life who think (or at least behave as if they think) that life is a one-time-around, one-way ticket with no second chances. Although those of the "go for the gusto" crowd are obvious examples, they may be but a small and vocal minority in a much more vast and silent majority. However, we all share (although some may not recognize our common bond), a problem: how to get the best that life has to offer in the time allotted. The six popular answers to Plato's big question are simple and easy and, on that account alone, appealing: "A type of life worth living is the life of _____." Fill in the one-word blank and you've got it! No fuss, no muss, no hard process of self-examination to strain the mind, no aporia, and no painful philosophic birth process. All you have to do is give a one-word answer and you're on your way to happiness and a life worth living. Easy, huh?

So why not take the easy way out? The answer to this question is ironically simple: it doesn't work. To embrace one of the six popular answers or any combination of them is to commit oneself

> **Platonic heaven:** Plato was inclined to believe that there is an afterlife, and he offered a weak argument by analogy in defense of this view, but his considered opinion was agnostic. Interested readers can examine his discussion in his dialogue the *Phaedo.*

to a lifestyle that is likely to miss the golden mean by a whole lot, sort of like a plane's missing its landing strip by a continent or two. People who dedicate themselves to such lives are by the nature of their choice self-interested, and they are susceptible to being obsessive-compulsive types, given to intemperance, either in the form of excess or deficiency, and doing themselves and others harm in the process.

A Happy Life: Read the Fine Print

To appreciate Plato's analysis of human happiness and his answer to his own big question, let's approach matters sideways, starting with animals and then working our way toward human beings and the human condition. Animals have souls, too. In the section on Plato's ethics, we noted that *anima* is a Greek word for "soul." To discover an animal's nature, you need only to observe its characteristic behavior (the window to its anima), and then, as it were, read backward, inferring what the soul's capacities must be. Dogs bark and cats meow but not vice versa because dogs have doggy souls that enable and characteristically produce barking and cats have kitty souls that enable and characteristically produce meowing. If one could implant a kitty soul into a dog like Growl (remember Growl?), then Growl would meow and chase mice. But the science of genetics hasn't as yet advanced far enough to allow for soul transplantation across species. The infamous cloned sheep Dolly seems to have the same kind of soul as her maternal cell. No human observer has heard her do anything but bleat—no neighs, barks, or meows have as yet emanated from her, and none are expected.

According to Plato all animal souls have an appetitive part. Animals want to live, eat, procreate, and protect their young. These desires make up part of their animal nature. We can call the characteristic behaviors that these desires induce "natural functions"—activities animals perform owing to their nature or, in other words, owing to the soul they happen to have.

To make an animal unhappy, you need only to prevent it from satisfying its natural functions.

Now we have a hot lead to follow regarding animal happiness. Even Inspector Clouseau of the Pink Panther movies would have a hard time bungling this one. Here's the insight in a nutshell: If failing to satisfy natural functions makes animals unhappy, then satisfying their natural functions in the right proportion will make them happy. This insight probably squares with ordinary experience. If you feed Growl regularly and give her some freedom to roam and to do what comes naturally to her (including having conjugal visits), she will probably be a happy and contented creature and a loving pet. Of course, overindulgence should be avoided because too much of a good thing can harm her. Dogs, after all, can eat themselves to death.

The Role of Reason

According to Plato, the human being, who is by nature a step up from an animal, has a tripartite soul composed of appetite, emotion, and reason. (Remember?) Since our appetites and some of our emotions stem from our animal nature, we are animals, too. What makes the human soul unique is reason. To be happy beings and to lead the life worth living, we, too, need to satisfy our natural functions in the right proportion. This task is not easy given the scope and sometimes competing nature of the natural functions we need to satisfy. We need food, shelter, health, sex, security, affection, courage, honor, and mental stimulation, to name just some of our needs. In some respects, the body and the soul are alike. The body is a whole composed of parts and organs that need to be organized and harmonized if the whole physical being is to function effectively. In the healthy body, much of the regulating required for harmonious functioning of parts and organs is as automatic as a thermostat regulating heat in a room. The job of maintaining a well-ordered and happy soul also requires regulation, a task that falls to reason, which acts as a moderator, tempering the three parts of the soul so that the various natural functions related to each part are satisfied in proper measure.

Plato's Scheme Depends on the Existence of a Right Proportion and Our Knowledge of It

Otherwise, our happiness would be based on sheer luck or guesswork! For Plato, knowledge is a necessary condition of happiness. So we've come full circle. His question about the life worth living motivates and leads back to his epistemology and metaphysics. His positing the existence of a world of forms outside space and time (a metaphysical theory) and his theory of recollection (an epistemological theory) are main parts of his reply to the Sophists' skepticism about knowledge and ethics. Together these two theories explain how reason can acquire the knowledge it needs to guide the soul to a life worth living. (For more on Plato's theory of forms, see the earlier sections on metaphysics and epistemology, or wait for the coming discussion of the forms in the Philosophy Hall of Fame, pages 105–106.)

The story does not end here, friend. Human happiness and the life worth living depend not only on the equanimity and harmony of the soul itself but on the person's condition in life as a whole. Plato thought that his account of human happiness and the life worth living needed to take into consideration the fact that the worth of human beings depends in part on their social role and condition. In the way that some masters are better than others at satisfying their pets' natural needs, societies and the governments that regulate them vary in how good they are at giving their citizens the opportunity and wherewithal to lead fulfilling lives. Such considerations led Plato to analyze social orders for two purposes: to see which social organization was most conducive to the type of life worth living and to determine what social role a well-ordered soul should adopt to be happy. As British rockers The Clash said, "We have to fight for our right to be free."

PLATO'S THREE SOCIAL CLASSES

Although social orders don't have souls, they are analogous in respects. Like the human soul, they contain parts. According to Plato, these parts consist of three social classes: rulers, guardians, and producers, which correspond respectively to reason, emotion, and appetite in the individual human soul. As human souls can be differentiated from animal souls on the basis of our capacity to reason, so individual human souls differ one from another on the basis of their natural ability to rule, fight, or produce. The society that is regulated so as to guide individuals into the roles for which they are best suited and most effective is likely to be a well-ordered society. Its parts work together in the right capacities and with the proper attunement to achieve the highest degree of efficiency. If its citizens accept their natural roles because as individuals they have well-ordered souls that make the wise and temperate decision to aspire to nothing more than what they do best by nature, then these souls maximize their chances for experiencing the fulfillment of their natural functions and for achieving happiness and the life worth living. Got it? Read it aloud. That helps.

> Order! The social order that Plato recommends is described in the *Republic*. See also his *Laws* for his later thoughts on government and the state.

Plato's Definition of Happiness and the Type of Life Worth Living

Plato said that happiness is the satisfaction of the natural functions in moderation in accordance with the regulation of reason.

Is Plato's answer to his big question better than the six popular versions? It is certainly different. The six rival answers state that one is leading a life worth living if one has wealth, health, love, long life, beauty, honor and fame, or pleasure. How to acquire these purported goods becomes the primary challenge. With these goods as goals, the individual's natural tendency is to turn outward toward the objects of desire and to the management of events and resources so as to acquire them.

Plato's answer turns the soul in the opposite direction—inward on itself so that it can know and regulate itself and in consequence function efficiently in satisfying its natural human needs. To regulate effectively, reason prompts such important and sometimes hard questions as

- What am I?
- Who am I?
- What is the type of life worth living for a being like me?
- What am I good at?
- What are my needs?
- How can they best be met?

- How can my conflicting needs be balanced and satisfied in the right measure?
- What should my relationship to society be?
- What role should I play?

This process of questioning is in effect an inner dialectic, a dialogue with oneself.

Plato saw dialectic as a means for stimulating the participant's awareness of the forms. If the process of self-examination succeeds, individuals recall the relevant forms and acquire knowledge of happiness and the life worth living in general; they can ascertain which course of action in a particular situation exemplifies moderation, and then they can and will act accordingly. Seen from this vantage point, Plato's scheme turns out to be a hierarchy of means and ends:

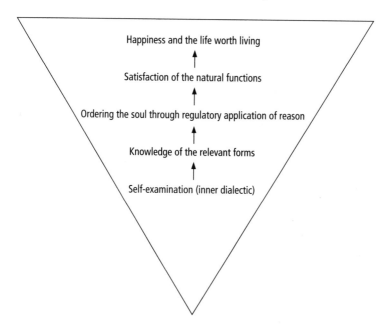

The practical task of satisfying natural functions requires a well-ordered soul, which knowledge of the right proportions can bring about. Without such knowledge, prescriptions for the life worth living are so much speculation. Much of Socrates' life and work in the agora was an effort to find out whether those who claimed to know what happiness and the life worth living are really knew what they were talking about. Almost invariably, they didn't.

The search for a life worth living wasn't restricted to urban Greeks, of course. In fact, the history of that search involves the philosophy of the soul, the philosophy of the self, and a dozen other subthreads, all of which cross and meet in varying degrees of entanglement. For example, Moses, in his effort to find the key to a life worth living, didn't bother with passersby. He went directly to the Source.

THE JUDEO-CHRISTIAN HERITAGE*

JUDAISM

"Hear, O Israel: The Lord our God is one Lord" (Deuteronomy 6:4). Talk about chutzpah! Moses called upon the Lord God to emancipate His people. In a spectacular demonstration of divine power, Yahweh heeded Moses' call, parting the Red Sea and uncovering the pathway for the Israelites to make their exodus to freedom. Imagine for a moment that you had lived over 3,000 years ago and had been among those chosen Israelites who walked unharmed through the walls of water and who witnessed the walls come crashing down on the pursuing Egyptian army and swallowing them up in a prophetic foreshadowing of the Six-Day War. Can you imagine yourself experiencing such an event and then forgetting it? And wouldn't you think you'd be really really *really* careful not to offend the Big Guy, who had the power to make that miracle happen?

Maybe it was the heat, maybe the monotony of wandering in the desert, maybe the steady diet of matzo, but when it comes to being fickle, the early Jews were undisputed hall-of-famers. As the story goes, Moses, acting as emissary of his people, climbed Mount Sinai to speak with God, who had willed that the Israelites should be favored with a covenant. In return for their obedience to God's decrees, He would make them His chosen people. Like a good ver-

---

*The *Pocket Professor*'s volume on Religion discusses this subject more thoroughly, if not more seriously. Much of theology is given to discussions of matters of textual interpretation so arcane as to amaze and befuddle the uninitiated. Given space limitations here, we cannot hope to disentangle these theological niceties. Besides, we're philosophers here. The good side of this limitation is that it leaves us with a license to levity, which we acknowledge having shamelessly exploited.

sion of a mob godfather, the Lord was offering Moses a deal he couldn't refuse.

Just so that there would be no misunderstandings about His intent, God etched His commandments into stone, which Moses brought down from the mountain, only to find his fickle flock worshipping a golden calf and performing such unspeakable and unclean acts that a very explicit contemporary film version of the event couldn't muster better than a PG rating, despite vocal support from religious groups who vigorously championed the epic on account of its biblical content.

In defense of Moses, we have to note that he was hot and tired. Seeing his flock sinning against God and the covenant that they had, without their knowledge, just entered into, Moses became angry and broke the stone tablets. God punished Moses by leading him to the Promised Land but not allowing him to enter.

Although this tale of law, crime, and punishment has influenced the Western psyche, Jews have tended to emphasize the law part over the crime-and-punishment part of the story. They view the law, which they elaborated into a complex and comprehensive system of jurisprudence governing large and small matters of life, as God's gift to His chosen people out of caring and concern for them. God understood the life worth living, and He told the Jewish people what it is—a life lived according to the law.

The good Jew is not obedient out of fear of God's wrath and punishment (although the Bible gives ample reason to be afraid) or out of hope of winning a heavenly afterlife. In fact, the afterlife plays a diminished role in Jewish life. Earthly existence is what counts most. Obedience to the law is its own reward; it makes life worth living for oneself and others. Through good deeds, the pious Jew betters humanity's earthly estate until the coming of the Messiah and, with him, the promised kingdom of peace, not in heaven, but on earth.

CHRISTIANITY

Although Plato and Judaism shared Christianity's belief in the immortality of the soul, the afterlife played a subordinate role in their interpretation of and answer to the big question. They were primarily occupied with finding a prescription for the earthly life worth living. Plato's answer was the golden mean; Judaism's was obedience to the law.

With Christ and his disciples, the center of gravity shifted away from the terrestrial and from the tug of things earthly. To followers of Christ, each soul is immortal and lives through two very different phases of life, a brief stint here on earth and an eternal life hereafter. Happiness in the afterlife depends on how earthly existence is lived. Fundamentally, the afterlife will take one of two forms: eternal bliss or eternal damnation. One might say, tongue in cheek, that eternal damnation is hellish. The traditional portrayal of this hell is an everlasting torture chamber of unspeakable and unremitting pain and anguish—an evocative way of explaining the circumstance of a soul deprived of the presence of God.

THE NAGGING QUESTION

According to Christianity, each person faces a momentous choice that can be expressed in the form of a question that is so often repeated that even the most dedicated nonbeliever cannot outrun it. The question is pervasive, like the sound of silence. It is written on the subway walls; muttered on the streets of any city; sung on Christian rock radio stations; put to the faithful and the wayward on the radio program *Family Bible Hour* in Anywhere, U.S.A.; or asked quietly by a Jehovah's Witness, Bible in hand and firmly planted on your doorstep. Put succinctly, the question is this: Would you rather pass eternity in everlasting bliss or eternal anguish?

Now, there's a no-brainer if ever there was one, or so you would think, but between the question, the answer, and the behavior that you'd expect to follow, there appears to be some sort of synaptic disconnect, an interruption and redirection of the flow of electrons along the neural pathways. Something goes awry. People who should know better behave in transparently Godless or at least un-Christlike ways.

For the Christian, the only life worth living is one with God. Earthly existence has only derivative value as a rite of passage by which one can earn one's reward in heaven. This circumstance leads to another question: What do I have to do while here on Earth to attain heavenly bliss hereafter? The answer is to be Christ-like, to make Christ your model and guide.

Christ's life had a divergent aspect: He preached unyielding attention to the life not of this world, yet he also intervened in the affairs of the world out of love for humanity. Christ renounced pleasures, pride, and pretensions as snares and delusions that turn us away from God and therefore from happiness. He spurns physical pleasures, fears no evil, turns the other cheek, exalts humility, and commends chastity and poverty. Yet he also is actively compassionate, embracing the outcast and ministering to the weak, the suffering, the lost, and even the oppressor. Although the two aspects of his life may seem to be steering him in opposite directions, the one away from the world and toward God and the other toward the world and away from God, at bottom they accomplish the same goal. Both redeem the soul by directing its attention outward, away from self-centeredness and occupation with selfish needs. In this way, the bonds to this world are loosened and the kingdom of heaven and the life worth living are ultimately won.

So earthly life for the Christian turns out to be like a coupon; it has no real worth until redeemed. Yet winning eternal bliss is not easy. For Christ, motivation—what is in your heart—is more important than what you accomplish through your action. A failed attempt at goodness counts more than a right act undertaken for the wrong reasons. Even a life that is modeled after Christ's can be mere mimicry. Devoid of genuine compassion, it will doom rather than save the mimic. Christ's sentiment toward the law is similar. Jesus was a Jew who embraced Jewish law for the most part. The law was essentially good, but blind obedience or obedience out of fear rather than love will not of itself win one a place in God's kingdom.

Obviously, to Christians, living with God in heavenly bliss is the life worth living, but to earn a place in heaven, you first need a heart filled with Christian love. What if your heart is impure and lacking in the love it needs? The solution is not as simple as pulling into your local love station and yelling, "Fill her up!" Some Christians believe that you can't put love into yourself simply by wishing it there; you need God's help, His grace. Others think you can achieve love through force of will and effort, and some recommend practicing the right behavior on the theory that the loving motivation will follow if one repeats righteous behavior long enough.

That's the bright side. The flip side of the Judeo-Christian tradition is considerably more grim. Here are two reapers of optimism—Arthur Schopenhauer and Friedrich Nietzsche—whose influence has had much to do with the way philosophers and writers and artists see the world today.

THE DARTH PHILOSOPHER

Darkman Does the Details, or Arthur Schopenhauer (1788–1860)

THE GRIM BIOGRAPHY

Arthur Schopenhauer's father was probably a suicide, and his mother, a renowned novelist of her day, was a vain creature. The relationship between mother and son was quarrelsome and tempestuous. Eventually, for their mutual benefit, they lived apart. But he would return for her fashionable soirées to mingle with her guests, among them the intellectual and artistic elite of freethinking and romantic Weimar, Germany.

One evening the great Johann von Goethe, a frequent guest, remarked to Frau Schopenhauer that her son would one day be famous. If ever the milk of mother's love had flowed from this lady's dugs, it had long since dried up. Barren of motherly affection, this *mutter* could easily have doubled for Snow White's malicious and self-centered stepmom, with the single exception that her malice fixed on her child's intellect rather than beauty. Enraged at the thought of her own offspring's living to rival her fame, she shoved the hapless lad down a flight of stairs. He bumped and tumbled down the steps; their relationship reached its final resting place at the bottom. After dusting himself and his dignity off, the young Arthur fired his parting and final barb at Mommy Dearest. She would, he snarled, be known to posterity only through him. He went on to pioneer a philosophy of pessimism—and, perhaps, revenge, since his prophecy proved true and has given rise to the widely held suspicion that his mother's crypt resembles an elegantly appointed French rotisserie with Madame Schopenhauer skewered and turning over eternally, spitting in her grave, as it were.

In a psychological sense, Schopenhauer's tumultuous relationship with his mother may explain his misogyny, to which he gave elegant philosophic expression in his essay "On Women." Talk about torment! The lusty youth was torn between loathing females and being attracted to them. He was, as he confessed, no saint.

At the age of 30, Schopenhauer published his most famous work, *The World as Will and Idea.* He predicted great success for it, but it was hardly noticed, and most of the edition was sold as scrap paper. Fuming over the world's indifference to his genius, he longed for a post at a major university, a pulpit from which he could preach his philosophy. But when finally he was invited to lecture at the University of Berlin, he brashly scheduled himself opposite Georg Wilhelm Friedrich Hegel, whom Schopenhauer regarded as an arch philosophic nemesis but who was also at that time the Western world's most renowned and influential philosopher. The outcome of the folly of Schopenhauer's monumental ego was predictable. His lectures were largely ignored.

As years passed, Schopenhauer retreated from the world, living out his final years as a paranoid recluse, refusing to be shaved by a barber and sleeping with a loaded pistol at his bedside. Yet recognition did not elude him altogether, and in 1858, on his seventieth birthday, congratulations arrived from all over the world. Two years later, he died.

SCHOPENHAUER'S BAD NEWS: THE PROBLEM OF EVIL

Having been treated to some of the more lurid details of Schopenhauer's life, one might be tempted to dismiss his philosophy on psychological grounds as the ravings of an unloved, disgruntled, disconsolate, and certifiable cuckoo, all of which may be true. Yet dismissing a person's philosophy because he happens to be nuts is an *argumentum ad hominem*—you remember, an argument against the person rather than his or her ideas. So let's turn from away from psychology to philosophy and to Schopenhauer's theories, beginning with . . .

. . . a critical analysis, which is intended to make way for his own positive philosophy. With Schopenhauer, this is sort of like sending a 300-pound lineman to open up a hole through which a more nimble, lightweight running back can burst and then turn up field toward the goal line. Schopenhauer's critical analysis consists largely of a blistering attack on prevailing Judeo-Christian beliefs, many of which are so entrenched in the Western mind as to have the character of the axiomatic.

One of Schopenhauer's biggest gripes with Judaism is the purported optimism of the Old Testament as expressed in Genesis—you remember: God created the universe in six days. At the end of each day's toil, God, who knows everything, surveyed His handiwork and judged it good—a divine judgment so brimming with inscrutability that Schopenhauer could neither swallow nor stomach it. He's a depressing guy, but it's not hard to see his point. Like every casual reader of the daily headlines or viewer of TV news, you have been witness to an almost unremitting succession of wars, murders, rapes, thefts, vice, deceptions, death, destruction, and disasters, human made and natural. Mirroring this daily fare, human history is an epic tale of warfare and bloodshed. In the face of all this aggregated misery, how, Schopenhauer wonders, could any fair-minded, rational, and objective observer of the creation arrive at God's conclusion? All this calamity is instead powerful evidence that the universe is the opposite of what God claimed it to be. It is not good; rather, it is fundamentally evil, Schopenhauer believed.

Schopenhauer's pessimism raises the traditional problem of evil in a radical way. Here's the problem:

- In the Judeo-Christian tradition, God is thought to be a perfect being whose perfection consists in part in being omnipotent (all powerful), omniscient (all knowing), and omnibenevolent (all good).
- A generally held belief is that any product issuing from this perfect being must itself be perfect, not only in design but in moral perfection.
- But could, for example, the God of Judaism and Christianity produce any child (not just a Jesus) who was a 10 when it came to physical design and appearance yet a 1—endowed with an extra Y chromosome, as it were—when it came to moral character? Could God create, in short, a human having a design flaw in its immortal soul?
- Presumably not. Since God is all good, He desires nothing but what is good; since He is infinitely wise, He knows how to build creations that are perfectly good, and since He is omnipotent, He has the power to build exactly to His own design specs. So any flaw in the moral fiber of the offspring bespeaks a flaw in God.
- On the basis of this analysis, God's creation can contain no evil.
- Yet evil appears to exist. Through the centuries, Jewish and Christian philosophers and theologians had developed remarkable and sometimes extravagant theories to explain how evil can appear to be part of creation without really being so.

Schopenhauer's claim that evil not only exists but is a fundamental and ineradicable feature of creation is a direct and radical attack on basic Judeo-Christian doctrine.

The big ditch: Now you may be willing to admit, perhaps reluctantly, that evil is part of the world. But Schopenhauer was not content with minor concessions. He wanted to go all the way out to the edge, stare down the abyss of brutal reality without flinching, and then, as if prodded by some unseen pitchfork, gleefully and maliciously spread himself out in a contrarian, headlong, swan dive. He was intent on turning Judaism and Christianity on their heads. He considered evil to be the real character of existence and goodness to be the appearance. In effect, goodness does not really exist (except in the rarest circumstances). There is virtually no ray of light in this bleak reality; pain and evil are virtually everywhere the rule. Goodness, you may protest, exists and in many forms: there is love, religion, the great chain of being (life in all its forms), art and beauty, a perfectly executed double play, and many noble acts of altruism, to cite some of life's saving graces. For you all this evidence represents a powerful refutation of Schopenhauer's belief in a fundamentally evil universe. Schopenhauer, however, would have replied with vigor and eloquence that these purported "good" things—with the notable exception of art and isolated acts of kindness—are really evil things in disguise.

SCHOPENHAUER IN LOVE

It's hard to look into the eyes of your own true love and think of Schopenhauer's evil empire.

Maybe it's too much Elizabeth Barrett Browning in your literary diet. To Schopenhauer, love is not the selfless caring of one person for another. It's about conflict. Strip away the glossy finish, says Schopenhauer, and you will find beneath the surface a bleak truth: Love is nothing but the battle of the sexes, the ongoing struggle of men and women for domination of each other. Regardless of how it has been expressed, the issue is and always has been the same: who will wear the pants in the family. In this warfare, Schopenhauer says, women are wiser and more adept. Because they are the physically weaker sex, they have cultivated sophisticated weaponry, feminine wiles, to which men in their ingenuous naïveté and openness are innocent prey.

According to Schopenhauer, by nature women are liars and deceivers who deploy their wiles in both the physical and the mental theaters of the battleground. Women feign interest in such male pursuits as football, bowling, and fishing in which they have no real

LIFE WITHOUT FATHER

Lionel Tiger's *The Decline of Males* describes the social and political effects of widespread use of contraception on the importance of men in women's lives. Arthur Schopenhauer's "On Women," which is to be found in his collection of essays *Parerga und Parilipomena*, is as short, compact, and elegantly composed a piece of misogynistic writing and thinking as the mind of Western man has ever devised. But he didn't see the long-term effects of controlling childbirth—and chief among them is a growing awareness that there *are* no marital responsibilities for men.

interest other than as a means to lure an unsuspecting man into thinking that he has found a genuine soulmate. But once a woman has snared her prey and trapped him in marital responsibilities, her pretense of interest wanes, leaving him with obligations in return for little reward. In the bowling game of life, the poor guy is never going to break 100 again.

Schopenhauer claimed that in the physical theater of the battleground, to arouse and attract the male of the species, women play on men's sexual impulses, adorning their bodies in fetching apparel to create an illusion that surpasses the reality. Then they apply cosmetics to disguise their blemishes, and finally they anoint themselves with perfumes, artificially created pheromones to arouse male sexual response. The simpletons' heads are so turned and befuddled that they come to see the female body as an object of unsurpassing beauty. As Schopenhauer put it in his flamboyant and malicious style, "It is only the man whose intellect is clouded by his sexual impulse that could give the name of *the fair sex* to that undersized, narrow-shouldered, broad-hipped, and short-legged race."

Schopenhauer didn't see romantic love as a shining example of goodness in an otherwise dark creation or as a gift of a rational, good, and loving divine intellect. As a form of warfare, according to him, it is as irrational and wicked as warfare and a scourge on the landscape of human existence.

NO SALVATION FOR PESSIMISTS

Schopenhauer considered the problem of salvation and found it silly. His reasoning: Augustine, a saint of the church, preached that most souls are predestined to damnation and can be saved only through God's intervention and grace. Thomas Aquinas, also a saint of the church, preached that each soul is free to choose and that one's choices determine one's fate hereafter. Popes, who are, according to Roman Catholic doctrine, infallible, have embraced with equanimity the teachings of both. To Schopenhauer's taste, this stewpot of Catholic contradictions, regardless of how subtly garnished, is fit only for the undiscriminating palate.

CREATION ACCORDING TO SCHOPENHAUER

According to the book of Genesis, God created heaven and earth, night and day, sea and land, and life in all its forms: plants, birds, fish, mammals, creeping things—in short, all the beasts of the earth, capped off with Adam and Eve. Although made in God's image, Adam and Eve and their descendants turned out to be incorrigible sinners, very unflattering and embarrassing likenesses of the Lord. God took it as long as He could; then He loosed the flood. Nothing survived except Noah's family and their shipmates. Later when the waters had receded, God commanded Noah to let the animals go so that they might multiply abundantly. God promised to never again destroy all life on Earth.

According to the conventional view held before Charles Darwin published his theory of evolution in 1859 in *On the Origin of Species* (one year before Schopenhauer's death), God, the Father of all things, gave each species the means of its own survival. The snow rabbit He made white so that the creature would be undetected in its snowy habitat. Deer were camouflaged a mottled brown so that they would be unseen in the forest. Mice were made fleet of paw so that they could scurry to safety, evading the millions of conspiratorial cats who lay in wait for them, and so on for every creature.

Viewed from this perspective, God's creation, taken as a whole, had the character of a great chain of being, a grand order and design for the harmonious and compatible preservation of the abundance and diversity of life. What greater testimony could there be of God's wisdom and love for all His creatures?

Schopenhauer saw this great hierarchy of life not as evidence of benign divinity and providence but as a colossal killing machine, each living creature sustaining itself by inflicting pain, suffering, and death on other frightened and hapless creatures. Top to bottom, the natural state of life is perpetual, unremitting, bloody, grizzly, and pitiless warfare, an endless struggle by each creature to survive at the expense of others. All creatures abide in a state of nature that Thomas Hobbes described aptly as "nasty, brutish, and short."

To dramatize this pessimistic outlook, Schopenhauer related a story he had read. A visitor to Java reported coming on a large plain that was covered as far as the eye could see with the carcasses of giant sea turtles. Each year these turtles emerged from the protection of the sea and made their way onto the beaches to lay and bury their eggs. Afterward, the wild dogs that inhabited the island descended on them and, working as teams, flipped the turtles onto their backs. Like high-powered and efficient paint strippers, they peeled back their victims' lower protective shields and ripped from their soft and defenseless bellies the living flesh of these parents-to-be. Schopenhauer concluded his narration with this parting reflection: "For this, then, these turtles are born."

According to Schopenhauer, the real character of God's gift of life is pain and suffering. At its core existence is fundamental and thoroughgoing evil.

HOW SCHOPENHAUER WAS SAVED

Schopenhauer did have a positive philosophical vision, believe it or not. For example, although humanity's fate, he told us, is pain and suffering, our lives are decidedly not worth the living, and our lot is just about hopeless, there is still the matter of will. Schopenhauer was a voluntarist. Voluntarism is the metaphysical theory that everything in existence has will or volition. Most readers will be inclined to dismiss voluntarism out of hand because it attributes will not only to living animals and human beings but also to rocks, lakes, air, and all objects generally thought to be inanimate and therefore presumably incapable of will. According to Schopen-

THE EGOTISTICAL HERO

Altruism is acting out of concern for others. But according to Arthur Schopenhauer, almost every purported act of altruism is not what it appears to be. To make his point clear, let's again use a contemporary example.

Suppose you observe an act that seems to you to be one of self-sacrifice. A total stranger flings himself in front of an oncoming vehicle to save a child chasing a ball into the street. The media, the American Legion, the Veterans of Foreign Wars, the state legislature, the governor, members of MADD (Mothers Against Drunk Driving), and inveterate paradegoers will proclaim his heroism from rooftops, hilltops, bars, beauty parlors, churches, synagogues, and mosques. Hardened and once unrepentant degenerates will weep and

hauer, the will, which is part of a thing's mental makeup and nature, motivates in part its public behavior. In this way, the will is, according to Schopenhauer, "objectified." It effects changes in the world that then stand out as public, objective expressions of inner desire. For example, imagine a prizefighter delivering a haymaker left to his opponent's unprotected head, turning his victim's once equine shnozzola 90 degrees to starboard. Thus transfigured, the twisted and unsightly snout constitutes objective and conspicuous evidence of the will of its owner's adversary, his inner drive. It is, as Schopenhauer said, an objectification of will. The nose knows.

According to Schopenhauer, not only does everything have will but all things have a certain kind of will—the will to live. Everything wants to preserve itself; everything wants to survive. Here's how it works:

swear off booze, drugs, sex, and crime at the mention of his name. To memorialize him, Little Leaguers will sport black armbands, and yellow ribbons will suddenly, *ex nihilo,* festoon trees as if some spectral Johnny Appleseed had busied himself in the dead of night applying free samples of Ribbon Gro to every tree root in town. Yet all this tribute is based on very flimsy evidence as to our hero's purposes. Motivation is, after all, interior. According to Schopenhauer, outside observers who judge behavior to be altruistic are almost always ignorant of the perpetrator's ulterior motivation. If one had the power to read minds and apprehend inner motivation, behavior would be revealed for what it almost always is—transparent and naked egoism.

- Because every creature wills to preserve itself and to do so at the expense of other creatures as circumstances may require, each is a potential threat or impediment to the survival of others.
- For each living being, every other creature assumes a sinister aspect, and, declared or undeclared, each creature is *de facto* in a state of cold or hot warfare of all against all. No wonder Schopenhauer was a paranoid nut sleeping with a loaded pistol next to his pillow.

All the suffering of the world, says Schopenhauer, has one root cause—the blind, irrational desire to preserve one's self. It is the will to survive that is the driving force, the engine, and explanation of all the evil, pain, and suffering of existence. Although unaware, we have all along been contributors to the calamities and the pain that afflict the world and ourselves as part of it. The question is, can we extricate ourselves from this predicament? For Schopenhauer, the answer was clear: The way to relieve the pain of existence is to defeat the will to live.

To answer this question, Schopenhauer drew on both Western and Eastern traditions: Plato and Immanual Kant representing the former and Hinduism and Buddhism representing the latter. As different as these sources are, they share a common metaphysical outlook based on the distinction between appearance and reality. According to each, our experience of the world is a mere appearance of and very different from fundamental reality itself.

How to Lose the Will to Live, Eastern Style

In the Hindu tradition, the world as it appears under ordinary circumstances is characterized variously as a play, a dream, or an illusion. A veil of *maya,* or illusion, conceals the fundamental reality from us. To reveal it, we must pierce the veil. In Hinduism and Buddhism, various practices have been recommended as ways to accomplish such a revelation.

How to Lose the Will to Live, Western Style

In the Western tradition, Plato and Kant (among others) attempted to give dualism a rational foundation. Although both Plato and Kant influenced Schopenhauer, Kant's influence was the more immediate and profound, with Schopenhauer adapting Kant's metaphysics to his own purposes.

IMMANUEL KANT'S METAPHYSICS

To help you understand Immanuel Kant, we will draw an analogy. Imagine that you are taking a picture of a dog using a Polaroid camera. Three distinct entities are involved: a pet dog, a Polaroid camera, and the photograph that comes out of the camera after the picture is snapped. Analogous counterparts to this trio are listed below in the right column:

Example	Analogous Counterpart
Dog	Fundamental reality
Polaroid camera	Mind (for Arthur Schopenhauer, the "intellect")
Photograph	World of appearance

The following is another way to illustrate these same relevant relationships:

Camera	Dog	Photograph
(mind or intellect)	(fundamental reality)	(world of appearance)

What's at work here:

- The photograph is the product of an interaction between the dog and the camera via the medium of light that reflects off the pooch in the direction of the Polaroid's lens.

- Existing independently of the camera, the dog remains unmoved and unaffected, the camera producing no alteration in him.

- Nevertheless, the resulting photograph contains a representation of him. He is present before the camera when it takes his picture, and it in turn re-presents him in the form of a figure on a two-dimensional, glossy, 2 × 3 black-and-white.

- The dog is, however, very different from the two-dimensional representation of him. He is three dimensional and large and has a dull brown coat.

- Yet the picture can be said to contain his appearance or likeness. It represents him even though he doesn't actually enter into, get processed by, or issue from the camera that depicts him.

- The representation that does issue from the Polaroid is contained in a photograph rather than, say, a musical composition, owing to the camera's specific organization and the processing it is designed to do. It turns out photographs rather than other things. According to Kant our minds, like the camera, interact with and represent a world. Three entities are involved:

  - The world as it exists in itself independently of the mind (the dog, a.k.a. fundamental reality)

  - The mind or intellect that interacts with the world as it exists in itself (the camera)

  - The representation, appearance, or likeness that issues as a result of the mind's or intellect's interaction with the world in itself and issues as part of our world of appearance (the photo, obviously)

The representation issuing from the mind's "camera" is our experience of the world; it is the world as it appears to us. The mind's organizing and processing activity is conducted in accordance with certain principles of design built into it.

E pluribus: For Schopenhauer, a main principle of organization is the principle of individuation, the principle that the world is composed of independent individual entities, distinct from each other.

Processing in accordance with his design principle, the mind represents the world as a divided and individuated reality, carved up into you, me, every other individual human body and will, individual dogs, houses, airplanes, insects, planets, atomic and subatomic particles, and all the other things that collectively make up the world as we know it.

But this representation of the world was for Schopenhauer a disastrous misrepresentation of fundamental reality, the world as it exists in itself. It turns out that the mind is an obsessive-compulsive trickster that organizes all its representations so that they will conform to the principle of individuation, a design characteristic belonging to the mind but with absolutely no bearing or effect on fundamental reality, the world as it exists independently of mind and its organizing principles and activity. According to Schopenhauer, the character of fundamental reality as it exists in itself is very different from the way it appears. In itself, reality is the will to live, an undifferentiated unity, an indivisible one in which no individual things or wills exist.

SCHOPENHAUER WENT TO INDIA FOR SALVATION

Once the intellect attains to that level of understanding which Hindu mystics achieved 4,000 years ago, it is put into a new and more tenuous relationship to its former belief system. All the striving of individual wills and all the pain and suffering caused by the belief that there are wills to fight against and a individual will to preserve is revealed as *sansara,* or illusion of mind. In reality, there are no individual things, and there are no individual wills, no you, no I, no one to preserve and no one to struggle against. For the Hindu and the Buddhist, life on that plain of existence in which we live our lives uncritically seems real, but it is isn't. The individuation of all things, the separation of all from all is a product of intellect, which misrepresents fundamental reality as a collection of separate and disconnected things, severed and distinct from each other. The truth of the matter is expressed in the ancient and holy Hindu expression *Tat twam asi* ("This thou art"). All things are one.

Armed with this knowledge, the soul is better positioned to begin its ascendancy to salvation. But to achieve this state, it needs to perform an act of will contrary to its nature—the renunciation of the world and with it the will itself. Now, this is a task of no small magnitude, and perhaps you are scratching your head about how to do it. Hindu and Buddhist teachers have preached manifold paths to salvation, including the Buddha's eightfold way for accomplishing the feat; Eastern Orthodox monks have embraced hesychasm as an alternative.

Let's say you succeed in finding a path to salvation and that you also succeed in calming and quieting your will and destroying the world-as-mind-represents-it and with it, your own ego. Then no thing—that is, nothing at all—remains to will with or for or to struggle against. The individual will will have vanished, giving way to a timeless nothingness, a state of peace, free of pain and suffering. (Of course, in the ordinary sense, you, your individual self, won't be around to enjoy it.)

This for Schopenhauer is the state of salvation; it is the life worth living, and it is his answer to our really big question.

Now for somebody *really* unpleasant.

THE AUTHOR OF UNHOLY UNHAPPINESS: A PESSIMIST'S PESSIMIST, OR FRIEDRICH NIETZSCHE (1844–1900)

THE GRIM BIOGRAPHY

A Lutheran minister, Friedrich Nietzsche's father died when his son was four, leaving the lad to be reared in a household of devout women in an environment of feminine delicacy and sensibility. His schoolmates dubbed him Little Minister, apparently a nickname chosen more out of puckishness than respect. At the age of 18, he repudiated their premature and, as it turned out, richly undeserved ordination, abandoning his faith altogether in favor of a dissolute life, during which time he may have contracted the venereal disease that was the likely cause of the insanity that deranged his final years.

FRED MEETS ARTHUR

At the age of 21, he read Schopenhauer, a source of early inspiration and later disappointment. Schopenhauer's account of nature as an irrational and bloody mechanism for the perpetual production of pain and suffering turned out to be a prophetic and remarkable precursor to Charles Darwin's theory of natural selection, made famous with the publication of *On the Origin of Species* in 1859, a year before Schopenhauer's death and 15 years after Nietzsche's birth. Schopenhauer's theory anticipated Darwin's views on the struggle for survival. But Schopenhauer was also an avid supporter of Darwin's predecessor, zoologist Jean-Baptiste Chevalier de Lamarck, who held that variation of species could be attributed to acquired characteristics, which could then be genetically transmitted to offspring. Darwin rejected the view that acquired characteristics could be inherited, but his theory appeared too late to influence Schopenhauer's written work.

Although Nietzsche admired Schopenhauer's audacity and the courage and fierceness of his attack on the prevailing and cherished values and traditions of his day, Schopenhauer, the worldly philosopher, was in Nietzsche's view just what he claimed to be—more appearance than reality, a tough nut on the outside but all soft and gooey inside. Like a crybaby rejecting one teat for another, Schopenhauer declared his own tradition barren while sucking up to the religions of the East in an effort to evade his own pessimism. Seeking succor, he in effect became a sucker.

NIETZSCHE'S BATTLEFIELD EPIPHANY

In 1870, when war broke out between France and Germany, Nietzsche yearned for military adventure and the chance to be part of the great events of his day, but his weak constitution and his aversion to the sight of blood disqualified him from military service, even as a medic. Nevertheless, he was witness to a striking example of will at work. As if under a spell, youth on both sides volunteered life and limb in defense of their respective homelands, a response at once so impulsive and curious as to inspire a revelation of sorts. Although the fundamental reality underlying existence is, as Schopenhauer preached, will, Nietzsche said it is not the will to live but the will to power—a blind and irrational drive to dominate others through the force and strength of one's own excellence and superiority. The will to power explained for Nietzsche what Schopenhauer's will to live could not, why human creatures, often hopelessly outmatched, compete in mortal combat for mates, to protect their young, out of national pride, from religious or political zeal, or out of philosophic conviction. All this pugnacity at the risk of self-preservation is evidence of a fundamental human drive to impose oneself on the world—to bend it to one's own desires, values, and beliefs—to shape it, so to speak, in one's image.

THE BIG IDEA

To Nietzsche, the human species is ill prepared for the struggle nature has in store for it. All animal creatures are outfitted with an instinctual apparatus for species survival. In fight or flight, animals act and react without thought. By comparison, humanity's survival instincts are few and paltry, forcing human parents to protect and indulge their offspring through a long period of maturation that is constantly growing longer. Devoid of horns, venom, fangs, fleetness, prodigious strength, or other natural weaponry, the human being survives instead by thought.

The Bible teaches that reason is a divine gift granted to human beings so that they might have dominion over all the creatures of the earth. Nietzsche disagreed. In his view, thought is not a grand and glorious gift of God; rather, it is an evolutionary aberration, sickness, and curse. Ouch! Thinking hurts my head.

EVOLUTION

Through pagan rites of combat and competition, the most excellent specimens of the species won the honors and the right to rule and dominate the weaker members of the tribe. In this now lost but, according to Nietzsche, better time, human instinct, social values, and the social order harmonized, resulting in a distribution of power that reflected natural values and virtues . . . but no longer. During the Christian era the entirety of the natural order turned topsy-turvy.

In the old order the weak were powerless to effect their will openly and forthrightly against the strong and victorious. Forced into subservience, their will to power turned inward where it lodged in the craw as a cankerous

CREATION ACCORDING TO FRIEDRICH NIETZSCHE

When human beings first evolved, they were like their immediate progenitors—natural creatures struggling to survive against other creatures and human enemies. In this natural state, the strong prevailed at the expense of the weak, and they did so without guilt or shame. Just as a shark swallows a weak fish or a tiger rends the flesh of its bleating prey, not only without pity or guilt but with unabashed and uninhibited joy and satisfaction in the hunt and kill, so human beings in their original state embodied a system of natural values that became enshrined in the ethos of pagan societies. For Nietzsche, pagan virtues included strength, skill in the hunt, pleasure in killing, a desire for domination, mercilessness, possessiveness, and rapacity—all natural expressions and behavior of a creature with a lust for life and all, in their time and context, good and noble traits.

resentment. This mass of human defectives and decadents, as Nietzsche liked to call them, became a slave society or herd, which stewed in its juice, nurturing ulterior motivations. Plotting and contriving in its own interest, the herd lay in wait for opportunities to overturn the natural order of things through a transfer of power from the most excellent to themselves.

THE INVENTION OF RELIGION

Prevented from challenging their masters openly, the herd had to revert to other means, such as infecting their souls with fear, guilt, and self-doubt. The herd invented religions that praised the natural conduct of the weak, calling it good, and condemned the natural conduct of the strong, calling it bad. Christianity is the most advanced form of what Nietzsche thought of as a slave religion.

FOUR REASONS WHY FRIEDRICH NIETZSCHE DESPISED CHRISTIANITY

- **It raises the weak.** Instead of worshiping robust, lusty, warrior pagan gods as their healthy, fun-loving, and life-affirming heathen ancestors once did, the Christians embraced Jesus, whom Nietzsche described as a dyspeptic and emasculated man-god who despised as the Devil's work everything natural, vital, and lusty. In contrast to the pagan gods, Jesus offered up as virtues what any free and natural pagan would despise—poverty, humility, chastity, and turning the other cheek, for example.

- **It suppresses the mighty.** According to Christian teaching, the virtues of weakness carry the promise of eternal happiness to the unfortunate but deny such rewards to their oppressors, who cannot hope to achieve everlasting bliss short of a spiritual conversion, which, it may come as no surprise, has the effect of limiting power within the confines of approved Christian conduct. Camels, we are told, can thread themselves through the eye of a needle more easily than any rich man can gain glory in the hereafter. Although the aristocracy might think themselves advantaged by birth, they are woefully deluded. The enslaved and the impoverished are the truly fortunate ones. Their lot on earth is suffering, but suffering is good. Although their reward is deferred, the poor shall inherit the kingdom of heaven. In God's mansion, a penthouse suite awaits them because poverty and turning the other cheek come so naturally to those who cannot be or do otherwise.

- **It punishes strength.** To its system of rewards, Christianity adds a system of punishments. The message is clear and uncompromising: Harm anyone or even think evil thoughts without contrition, and your punishment at the hands of the infinitely powerful, omniscient, and loving God of Christianity will be certain, excruciating, and eternal.

- **It grants salvation to the guilty.** Consistent with Pauline doctrine, Christianity reserves salvation for those who succeed in suppressing their evil impulses or, failing in this quixotic aspiration, as mortal flesh is bound to do, who have the Christian decency to become sick at heart, suffering guilt and repenting of their sins. In the Christian system of values, such a sickness of soul (as Nietzsche would describe it) is a virtue.

On the other hand, Nietzsche believed that evolution saddled humanity with a higher form of consciousness and thought, which through the machinations of the defective and decadent elements of society gave rise to conscience . . . and humanity was undone. Worming its way into the soul, conscience took up residence as the inner voice of the lowing herd, condemning selfish thoughts and deeds inimical to the multitude. Acting as guardian to the downtrodden, conscience pricked the wayward soul, imprisoning it in guilt. Now captives of inner doubt, once powerful and self-assured exemplars of the human species, became mere shadows of their former selves, slaves of slaves.

THE POLITICAL VERSION OF WEAKNESS

The political dimension of Christianity is, according to Nietzsche, democracy. When Christ rendered unto Caesar what was earthly but denied him the human soul, over which only God can have authority, he gave impetus to the democratic principle of the inalienable dignity of the individual person and by extension to the democratic values of freedom, equality, and fairness. This extension of spiritual freedom to political and social life completed an inversion of virtues. The ethics of the enslaved herd triumphed over the ethics of the free and virile pagan, yielding a victory of the weak and defective over the best examples of the species.

For Nietzsche, the natural system of values has been turned upside down:

- Modern human beings are at war with themselves.
- The satisfaction of natural desires now bears with it pangs of conscience and inner suffering.
- To the extent that conscience rules, human creatures come to despise their own nature; they are victims of self-hatred.

BORN TO BE WILD

Check out Hermann Hesse's *Steppenwolf* for a literary work that Friedrich Nietzsche's philosophy greatly influenced. The main theme is the contrast between the life of social acceptability and the life of the untamed wolf that resides within us.

Like the wolf caught in a steel trap, the human being can only free herself by gnawing off her foot. Yet self-mutilation cannot liberate her in a larger sense. The price of freedom is that the once proud predator becomes the prey.

GOD'S OBIT

Nietzsche's lament is that we are too far gone to recover the instinctual life and its natural, guiltless self-assurance. We are products of a social, political, and religious conditioning that runs too deep into our individual psyches and our collective consciousness. For a crabby, tough-minded philosopher like Nietzsche, the old religions—Eastern or Western—hold no peace, solace, or hope. They are the inventions of small, outmoded minds, motivated by resentment. "God is dead," he declares defiantly . . . not that he imagines that God ever really lived. His point is that the advance of science has made belief in God antiquated.

We are, Nietzsche believes, alone and forlorn in an irrational Schopenhauerian universe, and we have no way to recover a life worth living. Once, our ancestors at the dawn of humanity led such a life. Their actions and nature harmonized, and they acted without shame on their will to power and their natural human desires. They were free to pursue fulfillment and the life worth living for such creatures as we. But from the beginning, humanity was also flawed and destined to failure.

IT AIN'T OVER TILL IT'S EVOLVED

Nietzsche notes that evolution of species is an ongoing affair. *Homo sapiens* is not the end of species variation or extinction. Humanity was an evolutionary mistake that nature will correct in the course of time. A stronger species, more suited to its struggle for survival, will replace its progenitors. Although Nietzsche does not imagine that he will live to see this day, the vision of it is not a matter of indifference for him; it is a sustaining hope that some human couple will one day sire a new creature better than themselves, a human strain that resists society's imposition of conscience and guilt. This new human, this superior type, will be beyond Christian good and evil; it will be an *Übermensch* or "overman," a superman whose nature and behavior coincide in instinctive, harmonious, and shameless deeds. Then the natural state of humanlike creatures will have been restored and with it the possibility of human freedom, joyfulness, self-confidence, and self-love, and with these, the life worth living.

> **HOW HE *REALLY* FEELS**
>
> For Friedrich Nietzsche's most outright and sustained attack on Christianity and a discussion of the transvaluation of all values, read *The Antichrist* and *Beyond Good and Evil*. For his views on the loneliness of existence due to being alienated from one's nature and for his views on the coming of the *Übermensch*, read *Thus Spake Zarathustra*. All these themes also appear throughout the corpus of his writing.

AS FOR THE LIFE WORTH LIVING . . .

The good news is the bad news. Philosophic problems, our big question among them, are like beaver dams: Just when you think you're rid of them, they come back. For some reason, this remarkable cycle of philosophic resurrection seems to occasion more exasperation than epiphany. The main complaint seems to be based on economic principle. Hard work is supposed to pay off, at least in a capitalist society. If it doesn't, it's a waste of time. This deeply felt conviction threatens the livelihoods of academic philosophers, which explains why so many colleges have made their discipline a graduation requirement. Who would take it otherwise?

Anyway, that's the bad news. The good news is that no answer to our big question is likely to be the last one. So if Nietzsche bummed you out, don't despair. There's always more to the story.

TO BELIEVE OR NOT TO BELIEVE . . .

In the twentieth century, two main lines of thought emerged regarding our big question: Christian existentialism and secular humanism both seek to answer the question "What is the life worth living?"

KIERKEGAARD LOOKS FOR A LEAP

The roots of Christian existentialism can be traced to Denmark. Danish philosopher Søren Kierkegaard (1813–1855) lived a short and tragic life, dying when Nietzsche was 11 years old. Kierkegaard's works had little influence outside Denmark until the rise of the existentialist school of philosophy in the twentieth century. Existentialists claim direct descent from Kierkegaard—but they also count Arthur Schopenhauer and Friedrich Nietzsche among their philosophic ancestors.

HEADLINE: PHILOSOPHER CAUGHT IN BED, FEELS GUILTY

In an unguarded moment, Søren Kierkegaard succumbed to the sins of the flesh, his weak and wretched body slinking into bed with a prostitute. His secret was so awful, so unspeakable, that he felt compelled to end his engagement to the love of his life, Regine Olson, rather than lead a life of deception with her. Kierkegaard suffered alone. His torment led him to question both the science and religion of his day. For more on Kierkegaard's melancholy and his relationship with his father and Regine Olson, see his *Journals.*

Biographical Note

Kierkegaard's writing is intensely personal despite his efforts to disguise himself behind the many pseudonyms he used to sign his works. His father was a self-made man. Already old when Kierkegaard was born, he reared his son in a stern and demanding Protestant faith. The youth came to fear, love, and admire God as he did his aging father, but this mix of sentiments can be explosive, and it led in Kierkegaard to profound depression and intense self-examination. By twentieth-century standards, at least in many quarters, the young Søren might not have seemed an irredeemable sinner despite his failings. Mostly, he liked to party, and by his own account, he was a pretty popular guy among his peers.

The Religious History of Kierkegaard

To understand Kierkegaard's contribution to theology and the philosophy of religion, we need to hop a puddle jumper for a short flight back to the thirteenth century. Saint Thomas Aquinas (1225–1274) was perhaps the foremost figure in a theological tradition called natural theology. A generally held belief among natural theologians is that human beings were made in God's image, which is why as part of our nature we share modestly (unless guilty of intellectual pride) in God's rationality. When compared with God, we are, of course, relatively dull-witted. Nevertheless, the Creator saw fit to give us enough reason to allow our minds to discover rational grounds for faith. We have the God-given ability to prove that God exists and that It has divine attributes, such as omniscience, omnipotence, omnipresence, infinite goodness, and a providential nature. To this extent, according to Aquinas, intellect is a handmaiden of faith and informs it.

Aquinas advanced five proofs of God's existence, which remain part of Catholic doctrine today. But with the rise of science, these proofs came under attack, most notably at the hands of David Hume and Immanuel Kant. Until recently, their attacks made the prospects for the success of natural theology remote at best, so much so that Arthur Schopenhauer could level a blistering attack against religion and Nietzsche could declare with bravado that God is dead, virtually taking for granted that the question of whether God's existence could be proved had been settled once for all.

> **TO AND FRO**
>
> For Saint Thomas Aquinas' five proofs, check out his *Summa Theologica*. For David Hume's attack on leading proofs of God's existence, see his *Dialogues Concerning Natural Religion*. For Immanuel Kant's attack, see his *Critique of Pure Reason*. (Although Kant repudiated traditional proofs for God's existence, he advanced a proof of his own on ethical grounds. See his *Critique of Practical Reason*.)

In themselves these results were troubling for religion but not fatal. Whenever reason failed to produce a rational foundation for religious dogma, churches had always fallen back on divine mystery and faith. But the demands of faith were, according to Kierkegaard, much more excessive than the average light-hearted and unquestioning Christian might imagine. Consider what a Christian is asked to believe: that Christ died and rose, that Moses parted the Red Sea, that Jesus was born of a virgin, who was herself pure, and other miracles inherently so incredible that any person relying on reason would have to repudiate them out of hand as absurdities. An absurdity is not just false; it is an impossibility—like the existence of a round square.

Such dark thoughts led Kierkegaard to a crisis of spirit akin to the crises that Schopenhauer and Nietzsche had experienced. Schopenhauer's response was to seek comfort in Hinduism and Buddhism. Nietzsche's was to stand fast, living defiantly without God. Each made a decision. For Kierkegaard, the whole matter boiled down to a choice: an either-or.

Kierkegaard's Leap of Faith

Either one rejects God, or one embraces God. There is no in between. If Kierkegaard had heeded the dictates of reason, he would have abandoned faith and consigned himself to a life without meaning. If he forsook reason, he could affirm his faith, despite absurdity and doubt. Metaphorically, his life stood at the edge of a precipice, and he had only two choices: to step back or go over. The whole point of faith is to step beyond reason. So he chose a leap of faith, a passionate, unfounded, absurd, and ecstatic embrace of Christianity and Christ. Over the edge he flew.

> **THE JUMP**
>
> For more on Søren Kierkegaard, check out his *Concluding Unscientific Postscript* and his *Either/Or.* To appreciate Kierkegaard's influence on twentieth-century Protestantism, Catholicism, and Judaism, respectively, check out Paul Tillich's *Courage to Be,* Gabriel Marcel's *Tragic Wisdom and Beyond,* and Martin Buber's *I And Thou.*

Kierkegaard had a profound influence on the development of Western religious thought, affecting Protestant, Catholic, and Jewish thinking. In the twentieth century, other passionate believers, who would come to be known as Christian existentialists, followed him over the spiritual ledge. For these thinkers, faith is a personal choice, a matter of action rather than understanding, and its reward is a life worth living, a life dedicated to God in obedience to His will.

SECULAR HUMANISM

In the twentieth century, secular humanists took another direction:

- By and large, they accepted Nietzsche's repudiation of God but not his repudiation of humanity.
- They agreed that reason is not God's gift, but it is not an evolutionary aberration, either. Rather, it is an endowment that sets humanity apart from the other animals, giving us potentialities no other animal creature can aspire to or attain. We're special.
- They said that although no God exists to define or measure the life worth living for us, humans have the ability to forge such a life for themselves out of their own resources.

In short, secular humanism is a proclamation of human capability and a denial of human helplessness before God. A trifle arrogant, but if there is no God, then nobody's looking.

Ironically, Kierkegaard was a major influence over one branch of secular humanists, the atheistic existentialists like Jean-Paul Sartre and Albert Camus. They shared his skepticism toward rationality and science, and like him, they emphasized that life is made up of choices that must be undertaken without an adequate foundation in knowledge or reason. The objective is to be true to yourself, committing yourself wholeheartedly to something in which you deeply believe. As with Kierkegaard, commitment means taking a leap of faith, passionately devoting yourself to your cause. For Sartre and Camus, the specifics of the cause were not as important as one's sincerity in working for it. You might be moved to fight for an end to homelessness, for zero population growth, for racial equality, for reproductive choice, against it, for returning the Dodgers to Brooklyn where they belong, for banishing pornography from the internet, for sainthood for Larry Flynt, or for lowering the basketball hoop to eight feet. Whatever your project, if you are fully and earnestly committed to it, you are leading a life worth living sans God, according to Sartre and Camus.

HAPPY HUMANISTS?

For literary discussions of existential commitment, read Jean-Paul Sartre's *Nausea* and Albert Camus' *Stranger* and *The Plague*.

Many scientifically minded philosophers of the early and midtwentieth century, such as Bertrand Russell and John Dewey, have likewise been atheists. Although they did not embrace the existentialist tradition or disparage reason, they, too, were fully engaged in life and believed that a life worth living could be lived without God. Although they rejected main tenets of existentialism, they behaved like existentialists. In fact, Dewey championed many social causes, among them his admirable defense of academic freedom when the City College of the City University of New York, then known as the College of the City of New York, fired Bertrand Russell for what were called his indecent views regarding sex and marriage. Years later, Russell joined Sartre on the New Mobilization Committee, a group of activist intellectuals who opposed the war in Vietnam. Bertie, as his admirers affectionately called Lord Russell, was arrested many times for illegal protest despite his then advanced age.

OUTRAGEOUS?

Bertrand Russell's *Marriage and Morals* contains what he said that gave the good citizens of New York such a frightful case of moral indignation.

So where does all this leave you? As any self-respecting existentialist would tell you, with a choice:

- You can deny religious belief and live a life of anguish and despair alone and without God, like Nietzsche, like Schopenhauer before he renounced his will, and like Kierkegaard before he leaped over the edge.
- You can deny religious belief, embrace secular humanism, reject the existence of God, and forge a life worth living out of values and projects of your own choice and creation, like Sartre and Camus on the one hand or Dewey and Russell on the other.
- You can accept religious belief, like Kierkegaard, and go flying over the edge in an ecstatic leap and affirmation of faith, joining the likes of Paul Tillich, Gabriel Marcel, and Martin Buber in a personal and intimate relationship with God. *Or . . .*
- You can look on network TV for a life worth living, blow off philosophy as too depressing or demanding, and go about the business of existence.

It's your choice. We wouldn't dream of telling you what to do.

THE PHILOSOPHY HALL OF FAME

There are a million anthologies of the history of Western philosophy. The same names appear in almost all of them. It's like Cooperstown, except to get into this hall of fame, you first have to be dead, typically a pretty long time, and it doesn't matter how many sportswriters vote for you. Also, judging from the list, being white and being male helps, too, but a future roster is bound to show a wider spectrum of members. For example, the second part of the twentieth century showed a remarkable change in the diversity of people who pursue philosophy as a career.

SOCRATES
Greek
470?–399 B.C.E.

Purportedly, the oracle at Delphi declared Socrates the wisest Greek of them all. He earned this honor because he professed to know nothing. Instead he characterized himself as a gadfly or midwife, drawing out of others truths that lay hidden within. His method was to engage others in dialogue using what came to be called the Socratic method or dialectic, a process of asking question after question. Socrates was Plato's teacher, and Plato features him as the protagonist of dialogues that Plato wrote in his early and middle years. An Athenian court of Socrates' peers condemned him to death for atheism and corrupting youth. For his martyrdom, Socrates became a symbol of the philosophic quest for truth regardless of the consequences to oneself.

Recommended works: There aren't any; Socrates philosophized orally (see page 38).

PLATO
Greek
428–347 B.C.E.

Plato grew up in the aftermath of Sparta's defeat of Athens. This humiliation confirmed Plato's belief that democracy, an Athenian invention, was a flawed political system that did not provide an environment conducive to the life worth living. His most important and influential theory is his theory of forms. The theory is an attempt to explain how we acquire knowledge. Plato argued that there must be two worlds, the world of particulars (sometimes called the world of appearance), which we inhabit, and the world of forms, which is a changeless world existing outside time and space. Plato theorized that our souls inhabited the world of forms during a pre-existence.

Apprehending the forms, the soul acquired all its concepts and knowledge, which it carried into its existence in this world. This theory comprises the basis of Plato's rationalism, his belief that all knowledge is acquired before birth. (See pages 39–41.)

Recommended works: *Republic; Laws; Phaedo; Meno*

ARISTOTLE
Greek
384–322 B.C.E.

Aristotle is the *Pocket Professor*'s pick for the most influential thinker on the development of Western thought. His theories in physics and astronomy went substantially unchallenged for nearly 2,000 years and his biology and logic were regarded as canon for more than two millennia. He was also a seminal influence on such diverse disciplines as political theory, ethics, the arts, aesthetics, jurisprudence, and rhetoric. Even today, despite the emergence and progress of science, most laypeople uncritically and unwittingly hold an Aristotelian view of the world, at least in broad outline.

According to Aristotle, the world is made up of individual substances, which are just things: the stones, automobiles, Hula Hoops, Beanie Babies, orangutans, reptiles, and people that populate our existence. Each thing is, according to Aristotle, a unit of formed matter, a material thing that also has form. Its form consists of its various characteristics and purpose. Aristotle deployed his analysis to advance an alternative to Plato's theory of forms. According to Aristotle, each thing's form is part of that thing and therefore part of the here-and-now world we inhabit. Plato did not have to invent a world of forms to account for knowledge. Aristotle's more down-to-earth metaphysics formed the basis for his empiricism, his belief that knowledge derives from experience. (See pages 41 and 50–54.)

Recommended works: *Metaphysics; Nicomachean Ethics; Politics*

SAINT AUGUSTINE
North African
354–430 C.E.

At the age of 34, Saint Augustine experienced personal revelation and embraced Christianity. In his *Confessions,* he recounts his personal struggle to find faith in a world that is God's creation yet manifestly includes evil. To explain the existence of evil, he borrowed from Plato, modifying Plato's philosophy to fit Christian doctrine. For Plato, the source of reality, knowledge, and value was the form of the good. In Augustine's adaptation God, as creator, plays this role. Its creation is divided into two cities: the city of the saved (heaven) and the city of the damned (hell). Before consignment to one or the other, human beings inhabit an earthly existence in which the future residents of heaven and hell in at least one sense cohabitate— that is, they commingle. According to Augustine, each individual's fate depends on faith, which in turn depends on divine grace.

Recommended works: *Confessions; The City of God*

SAINT THOMAS AQUINAS
Italian
1225–1274

Saint Thomas Aquinas Christianized Aristotle's philosophy, giving the church a corpus of well-developed Greek thought about the natural world and about human beings as natural creatures. Previously, the corporeal world had not been emphasized in Christian thinking, partly because occupation with the physical realm would have been viewed as a diversion of the mortal soul away from God. The crucial factor in readiness had been faith, not intelligence or understanding. Thomas embraced a moderated view. As a practitioner of what is called natural theology, he held that God had given human beings intelligence so that reason, which He thus dignified, might be used to inform and supplement faith. Borrowing from Aristotle and Plato, Saint Thomas used his reason to advance five proofs of God's existence as well as proofs regarding God's essence.

Recommended work: *Summa Theologica*

THOMAS HOBBES
English
1588–1679

Thomas Hobbes believed that Galileo's scientific method, which was proving so successful in physics and astronomy, could be extended across the full panoply of human inquiry. He advanced materialism, the metaphysical theory that reality is composed exclusively of three types of matter: physical bodies, human bodies, and the body politic. Changes in each could be explained in terms of laws of motion. Regarding the body politic, he held that humans in their original state on earth were in a state of nature or warfare analogous to the state of moving bodies colliding with each other. Although sovereign in the state of nature, each person endures a life Hobbes described as "nasty, brutish, and short." Out of self-interest, people enter into what came to be known as a social contract in which individuals give up autonomy for peace and order. According to Hobbes, the best political organization is absolute monarchy. (See page 35.)

Recommended works: *De corpore* (Concerning Body); *De homine* (Concerning Man); *Leviathan*

RENÉ DESCARTES
French
1596–1650

René Descartes is often called the father of modern philosophy. His philosophy was an attempt to reconcile science and religion. He began by systematically doubting his former beliefs with the intent of subsequently rebuilding the corpus of human knowledge on a new and firmer foundation. Through this process, he discovered what he believed to be an indubitable truth: "I think, therefore I am" (*Cogito, ergo sum* in Latin). On the basis of this truth, he mounted proofs of the existence of the individual mind as a thinking substance, of God's existence, and of the existence of the physical world. According to him, existence is composed of two fundamental types of reality: matter and spirit. This metaphysical dualism gave rise to a philosophic legacy known as the mind–body problem: How do two fundamentally different orders of reality—mind and body—affect each other? (See pages 29–30.)

Recommended works: *Discourse on Method; Meditations*

BARUCH SPINOZA
Dutch
1632–1677

Baruch Spinoza attempted to use Euclid's method, so successful in geometry and science, to bring philosophy and science together in an all-embracing unitary body of knowledge. According to Spinoza, only one type of substance, absolute substance, or God, exists. He conceived of God and nature as one. Although God is a unitary being, It has an infinite number of attributes or essential features. But the human intellect can apprehend only two of them—thought and extension. In treating thought and extension (the essence of matter) as attributes of the one and only substance, Spinoza circumvented Descartes' mind–body problem.

Recommended works: *Ethics*

GOTTFRIED WILHELM LEIBNIZ
German
1646–1716

Gottfried Wilhelm Leibniz theorized that the universe is made up of monads, infinitesimally small units of force, each with an individual purpose of its own yet each harmonized according to a preestablished harmony that God in Its goodness ordains to create the best of all possible worlds. Leibniz's theory dissolves that ol' mind–body problem. Since only monads, which are psychic units of force, exist, Descartes' mind–body problem concerning the relationship of minds to bodies extended in space does not arise.

Recommended works: *Monadology; New Essays on Human Understanding*

JOHN LOCKE
English
1632–1704

John Locke was an influential political philosopher and the first of a group of thinkers who came to be known as the traditional British empiricists. He declared that all knowledge derives from experience, and he attempted to show that none of our ideas are innate. The mind, he held, is at birth a tabula rasa, a blank slate on which experience writes. Using an introspective method, he went on to account for how we acquire our ideas by experience alone. Locke's theory gave rise to the egocentric predicament, the question of how we could know that a world exists outside us that has the qualities Locke attributed to it on the basis of experience and the physics of his day. Locke noted that we experience sensations that we do not will to have in us. For Locke, the natural conclusion was that the external world exists and is the origin of such sensations.

Recommended works: *An Essay Concerning Human Understanding; Two Treatises of Government*

BISHOP GEORGE BERKELEY
Irish
1685–1753

The second traditional British empiricist, Bishop George Berkeley, subscribed to a metaphysics called idealism, according to which only minds and their ideas and affections are real (see page 36). He rejected the theory that an external material world exists. "To be," he said, "is to be perceived." Locke had attempted to demonstrate the existence of the external material world as the origin of ideas of sensation in us. Berkeley agreed with Locke that our ideas of sensation had to have an external cause, but that external cause did not need to be the material world. God, an immaterial spirit, could have put all our ideas in us. Berkeley thought this theory preferable because it averted the mind–body problem. For Berkeley, mind–body dualism was not a problem, because according to him, there are no bodies. God, a spirit, puts ideas into human minds, which are spirits, too.

Recommended works: *A Treatise Concerning the Principles of Human Knowledge; Three Dialogues Between Hylas and Philonous*

DAVID HUME
Scottish
1711–1776

David Hume was the third of the trio of traditional British empiricists. A main part of his critical analysis focused on the law of cause and effect. In the history of philosophy, the law had played a pivotal role in proofs of the existence of God, nature, and other selves. Systematically, Hume demonstrated that the law could not be rationally justified on empirical grounds. His skeptical conclusion brought into question the soundness of all the proofs that had relied on the law. On the basis of empiricism, he could have knowledge of occurrent experiences and memories, but he could not rationally justify belief in God, nature, other selves, or even his own self.

Recommended works: *An Enquiry Concerning Human Understanding; A Treatise of Human Nature; Dialogues Concerning Natural Religion*

IMMANUEL KANT
German
1724–1804

Immanuel Kant attempted to save science and faith from David Hume's skepticism. An analogy will help you understand Kant's reply. Imagine an old-fashioned but nevertheless automated meat grinder. If you drop cubes of beef into its top opening, it activates. What exits the other end is not the same as what entered; it is beef, but beef transformed from cubes to strands. To exit, the beef must first pass through a grate with round holes of a certain diameter. In addition to the internal process of grinding, these openings determine necessary features of what issues as the end product—not cubes, for example, but strands of beef.

To grasp Kant's theory, think of the mind as analogous to the meat grinder. Our senses, which according to Kant are part of the mind broadly conceived, interact with the world outside us. This interaction produces sensory stimulations that are funneled through the processor of our minds. The product issuing at the other end is our experience, which like the beef has and must have uniform features. But in the way that we do not directly observe the inner workings of the meat grinder as it processes the beef, we do not experience the workings of our senses or the inner workings of our intellect as they process the raw material passing through them.

These processes take place at an unconscious level. Yet we can infer on the basis of the uniform features that the end products exhibit what must have been going on inside the grinder and inside our minds. In the case of the beef, the grinder always issues strands; in the case of experience, it always issues in a world of causes and effects. According to Kant, our experience is the product of the organizing activity of our own minds. (See pages 58–63.)

To Kant, objective reality can be known only as it conforms to the essential structure of the organized mind. But this world of experience, which Kant named phenomenal reality, is not the only one.

He also affirmed the existence of a second world—the world as it exists in itself—apart from interaction with the mind. This world Kant called noumenal reality. If God, freedom, and immortal souls exist, they cannot do so in phenomenal reality, which conforms without exception to the law of cause and effect. There is no room in phenomenal reality for God's or humanity's free will. However, it is possible that God, freedom, and immortal souls exist in noumenal reality, which is independent of mind and the laws mind imposes including the law of cause and effect. Unfortunately, according to Kant, the human understanding cannot attain knowledge of noumenal reality, which by definition is reality that exists independently of the mind. So for us God, freedom, and immortality are only possibilities, which, Kant argued, we must postulate to make sense of our ethical experience.

Recommended works: *Prolegomena to Any Future Metaphysics; The Critique of Pure Reason; The Metaphysical Principles of Morals; Critique of Judgment*

GEORG WILHELM FRIEDRICH HEGEL
German
1770–1831

Georg Wilhelm Friedrich Hegel rejected Kant's metaphysical dualism.

According to Hegel, what is real is phenomenal reality or experience. Experience exhibits a duality: it involves both activity of mind (ideas) and what these ideas represent, which often has the character of pointing to something outside and independent of the mind. Although we can contemplate these two aspects separately, they are in fact inextricably connected. Because Hegel believed that nature has no existence independent of mind, he was an idealist (see page 36 for an explanation of idealism). Whatever is, according to him, is experienced and can be known. But knowledge does not require fixed categories of mind as Immanuel Kant had supposed. Rather, according to Hegel, mind and nature mutually develop according to a fixed process of dialectic. Every belief is a representation, a thesis, of how things are. According to Hegel, each belief has an opposite, an antithesis, to which it gives rise. To resolve the conflict between thesis and antithesis, a synthesis is formulated that incorporates both thesis and antithesis in a broader and more adequate understanding of reality. In turn, this synthesis becomes a new thesis, which gives rise to yet another antithesis, and so on until all knowledge is unified in a comprehensive picture of reality, which for Hegel was the absolute, or God.

Recommended works: *The Phenomenology of Mind; Encyclopaedia of the Philosophical Sciences in Outline; Science of Logic; The Philosophy of History*

JOHN STUART MILL
English
1806–1873

John Stuart Mill was an important contributor to ethics, political philosophy, logic, and scientific method. He defended a version of utilitarianism according to which the right course of action is the one that conduces to the greatest good of the greatest number (see pages 57–58). Although he believed democracy the best form of government, he cautioned against excesses. The majority has the potential to oppress the minority, and government can, at the expense of individual liberty, assume more expansive powers than is necessary to prevent harm to others. In matters of logic and knowledge, Mill was an empiricist who formulated rules for induction, a method by which generalizations could be inferred about the world on empirical grounds.

Recommended works: *Utilitarianism; On Liberty; On the Logic of the Moral Sciences*

ARTHUR SCHOPENHAUER
German
1788–1860

Arthur Schopenhauer is known as the philosopher of pessimism. He argued that the universe is fundamentally evil and not the product of an all-good creator's genius. The driving force behind the evil of the world is the will to live. Borrowing from Hinduism and Buddhism, he counseled that salvation depends on suppressing the will as the source of evil. (See pages 81–93.)

Recommended works: *The World as Will and Idea; Parerga und Paralipomena*

FRIEDRICH NIETZSCHE
German
1844–1900

Friedrich Nietzsche believed that the fundamental force in reality is the will to power. In the historical struggle for survival and domination, the natural order of the strong dominating the weak was reversed. Deploying intelligence to arouse guilt, the weak were able to enfeeble the strong, making them unable to force their will on others without remorse. This reversal of natural roles brought about an inversion of values. Natural pagan ethics gave way to Christianity and the Christian values of love and humility, which reflected the interests of the weak and defective. Nietzsche looked forward to the day that evolution would give birth to an *Übermensch* or superperson, who would pitilessly overthrow Christian values restoring the natural order of dominance (see pages 93–99).

Recommended works: *Beyond Good and Evil; Thus Spake Zarathustra; Twilight of the Idols; The Antichrist; The Genealogy of Morals*

JOHN DEWEY
American
1859–1952

John Dewey was one of the founders of American pragmatism, along with C. S. Peirce and William James. For Dewey, intelligence was an instrument of adaptation to a changing environment. Influenced by Georg Wilhelm Friedrich Hegel, Dewey believed that intelligence was developing along with scientific understanding of the world. Scientific methodology results in self-correcting theories and conceptual frameworks that, when current, represent humanity's best understanding of the world. Owing to the self-correcting nature of science, scientific theories are always provisional and fallible.

Recommended works: *Reconstruction in Philosophy; The Quest for Certainty; Experience and Nature*

BERTRAND RUSSELL
English
1872–1970

Bertrand Russell believed that modern science, coupled with recent findings in logic, could buttress, modernize, and revivify David Hume's empiricism. He was one of the pioneers in the development of the analytic tradition. Analytic philosophers believed their primary task to be critical analysis. Philosophical problems had notoriously suffered from obscure formulation. By clarifying the problems through language analysis, the analytic philosophers believed they could dissolve them, cleanse philosophy of obscurantism, and make it a handmaiden of science.

Russell believed that the world is made up of facts. The truth is a correspondence between propositions describing the facts and the facts themselves. A true theory would consist of a set of atomic propositions, propositions that are not amenable to further analysis. Science, not philosophy, is the appropriate enterprise by which to ascertain whether such atomic propositions accurately represent the facts.

Russell collaborated with another British philosopher, Alfred North Whitehead, to demonstrate that logic was the general form of mathematics. In the course of carrying out this project, Russell and Whitehead developed a logical language called the predicate calculus, which Russell and other analytic philosophers applied to long-standing philosophic problems in order to dissolve them.

Russell was also influential in social and political philosophy and a critic of religion, Christianity in particular.

Recommended works: *Our Knowledge of the External World; An Inquiry into Meaning and Truth; The Analysis of Mind; Why I Am Not a Christian*

JEAN-PAUL SARTRE
French
1905–1980

Jean-Paul Sartre was a leader of the existentialist movement. He believed that human beings are different from any other form of beings, whether inanimate or animate. The essence of human beings is freedom. In the case of human beings, existence precedes essence. We are born into the world without an essence or nature that predetermines what we are or what we will become. Likewise, God does not exist, so no divine purpose exists to guide our way. As human beings, we are, as Sartre said, condemned to be free. Our life is what we choose to make it, and from this condition there is no escape. We have no choice but to choose. By choosing our projects, we choose ourselves, selecting and defining the persons we are. Because our future depends entirely on us, we are responsible for it. Blaming bad luck, history, the environment, or causes beyond our control is all so much excuse making. It is disingenuous, or what Sartre called bad faith or lying to oneself. Like Socrates, Sartre recommended being true to oneself as the life worth living.

Recommended works: *Being and Nothingness; Existentialism and Humanism, No Exit*

Index